INSIDE
OUT

INSIDE
OUT

DR. LARRY CRABB

NAVPRESS®

Bringing Truth to Life

OUR GUARANTEE TO YOU

NavPress
P.O. Box 35001
Colorado Springs, Colorado 80935

The Navigators is an international Christian organization. Our mission is to reach, disciple, and equip people to know Christ and to make Him known through successive generations. We envision multitudes of diverse people in the United States and every other nation who have a passionate love for Christ, live a lifestyle of sharing Christ's love, and multiply spiritual laborers among those without Christ.

NavPress is the publishing ministry of The Navigators. NavPress publications help believers learn biblical truth and apply what they learn to their lives and ministries. Our mission is to stimulate spiritual formation among our readers.

Library of Congress Catalog Card Number: 98-11333

NAVPRESS, BRINGING TRUTH TO LIFE, and the NAVPRESS logo are registered trademarks of NavPress. Absence of ® in connection with marks of NavPress or other parties does not indicate an absence of registration of those marks.

ISBN 1-57683-082-9

Cover Photo by Adam Jones/Natural Selection, Inc.

Some of the anecdotal illustrations in this book are true to life and are included with the permission of the persons involved. All other illustrations are composites of real situations, and any resemblance to people living or dead is coincidental.

Unless otherwise identified, all Scripture quotations in this publication are taken from the *HOLY BIBLE: NEW INTERNATIONAL VERSION*® (NIV®). Copyright © 1973, 1978, 1984 by International Bible Society. Used by permission of Zondervan Publishing House. All rights reserved.

Crabb, Lawrence J.
     Inside out / Larry Crabb. —Expanded 10th
anniversary ed.
        p. cm.
     Includes bibliographical references.
     ISBN 1-57683-082-9 (pbk.)
     1. Christian life.   I. Title.
BV4501.2.C687 1998
248.4—dc21   98-11333
                                                        CIP

Printed in the United States of America

4 5 6 7 8 9 10 11 12 13 14 15 / 08 07 06 05 04 03

Published in association with Sealy M. Yates, Literary Agent, Orange, CA 92668.

CONTENTS

To My Two Sons,

KEP and KEN

*whom I love with a passion
that time only strengthens.*

*My greatest privilege and deepest
prayer is to be used of God
to further the wonderful process
of your growth in Christ.*

ACKNOWLEDGMENTS

This is the first book I've written under the pressure of a deadline—and I almost met it. Had it not been for the help of many people, I would not have come even close.

My wife and I spent a week with my sister-in-law and her husband, John and Ann Martin, at their lovely lake home in New York. They graciously endured an unsociable guest who wrote half the night and slept till noon. As the deadline neared, we went away for a few days with special friends, Mike and Becky Grill. Although I managed a round or two of golf, I spent most of the time writing while Mike took the ladies sightseeing—and he never complained. Thanks to both couples.

No one has a better friend or more trusted colleague than I have in Dr. Dan Allender. He sat still while I read aloud the first drafts of lengthy portions of the book (he could never have deciphered my scrawl), and gave me invaluable feedback. My thinking has been shaped during countless hours of dialogue with Dan about our lives, the Scriptures, the process of change, and a wide range of other topics.

My father deeply encouraged me with the comment that the message of this book is needed in today's world. Very few older men face their lives realistically and still cling passionately to

Christ. Most are either realistic and disillusioned or believing and defensive. Because he is both honest about life and rich in faith, I listen when he speaks.

Patty Warwick typed the entire manuscript from yellow pages filled with green ink that only her well-trained eyes could interpret. Her spirit was always cheerful. She worked hard, feeling the pressure of the deadline along with me. I'm very grateful.

Traci Mullins has earned my deepest gratitude and sincere respect for her editing. I turned in a rough manuscript, and she polished it into its present form. She had the wisdom and integrity to challenge me on difficult points and the sensitivity to encourage me along the way. Her personal involvement with the material and her unusual talent as an editor combined to make her an indispensable colleague in this project. My warm thanks for a new friend and a perceptive editor.

Rachael, my wife, endured a preoccupied husband without complaint. More than that, she demonstrated again that she is for me as only a godly woman can be for her husband. The pressure of writing created opportunities for rich movement in our ability to deeply touch one another.

Many others deserve thanks: colleagues at Grace Theological Seminary for encouragement and stimulation; the staff at NavPress for their support and excitement; and students in our counseling program for sharing their lives with me.

I pray this book will help us better understand what it means to really change so we can become increasingly like our Lord. Nothing matters more than knowing God. May we be deepened in our relationship with Him.

AN INTRODUCTION TO THE 10TH ANNIVERSARY EXPANDED EDITION

Ten years ago I picked up my pen and wrote, "Modern Christianity, in dramatic reversal of its biblical form, promises to relieve the pain of living in a fallen world." That sentence began this book in its first edition. It begins this revised one as well. My burden then was to return us to real Christianity where it is okay to hurt and where sin is a bigger problem than we think, where against the backdrop of inescapable groaning and unmanageable sin the gospel shines with all the brightness of heaven. That burden continues today.

Very few Christians feel their disappointment with life deeply enough to fix their hope on what is yet to come. Even fewer face their sin so thoroughly that forgiveness becomes their most valued blessing. But most Christians vaguely sense that they long for so much more than what they experience on a daily basis, and they suppress a terror that no one could know them fully and still want to be their friend.

Maybe that's why the book hit a chord. The message of *Inside Out* is simply this:

Feel the deepest longings in your soul that will never be fully satisfied till heaven. *Don't be afraid of sadness.* Face the hidden sin in your heart that makes it clear how thoroughly undelightful you are. *Don't be afraid of brokenness.* Let the pain of disappointed longings and the guilt of terrible sin drive you to consider the gospel of God's grace in a new way. Only then will Christ enter your life deeply and change you from the inside out, instilling in you a growing awareness of His relentless, unfailing love and a sustaining hope for a better day.

I believe the message of *Inside Out* is even more vital today than it was a decade ago. Of all the books I've written, this one has generated the most mail. A few think I should forget about deep longings and self-protective sin and simply instruct people to do whatever the Bible says. But that message is another gospel, a poor substitute that reduces Christian living to mere conformity and robs it of its richest fare: the enjoyment of grace.

Some others wish I would more clearly advocate psychotherapy as an often necessary element in provoking real change. But the core issues that I believe must be addressed if real change is to occur boil down to two questions:

1. Does anyone love me with the power to satisfy my soul? What is the object of my deepest desire?
2. Can anyone love me as I really am—self-centered, self-deceived, and self-righteous?

The work of change involves answering these two questions biblically and well. If that's what psychotherapy does, then I'm for it. However, I know that for one hundred years, we westerners have thought that peace and joy depend on personal "wholeness." We've assumed that difficult relationships, particularly in earlier years, have caused psychological damage that we label as mental disorder. The hope of heaven and the forgiveness of sins and the work of the Holy Spirit are thought to address spiritual problems; but real change, the kind that helps us feel whole and healthy, requires professional help. We need to be fixed by therapy.

So we *diagnose* people.

> ➤ A long-time friend admits to holding a grudge over a thoughtless remark five years ago. She may be evidencing the beginnings of a Paranoid Personality Disorder.
> ➤ A temper problem might point to difficulties with impulse control, perhaps an Intermittent Explosive Disorder.
> ➤ A girl in her late teens who still thinks about her boyfriend after he ended a two-year courtship could be suffering from an Obsessive-Compulsive Disorder.
> ➤ A middle-aged wife decides she can no longer handle the pain of her marriage to a neglectful husband. Her screams for attention through uncharacteristic behavior like drinking and over-spending would likely be diagnosed with Histrionic Personality Disorder.
> ➤ A few sleepless nights might signal the onset of a Major Depressive Disorder.

According to this line of thinking, psychotherapeutic treatment for the mental disorder is the only remedy, just as smooth skin can emerge only after chemotherapy burns off the diseased surface.

But the comparison doesn't hold. Psychiatric labels direct attention away from the real issues that must be addressed if spiritual fruit is to grow. We are not psychologically disordered; we are sinful people who believe lies about what must be ours in order to experience fulfillment. When the goals we set are blocked, we get mad. When they are uncertain, we worry. When we realize that nothing we do will help us reach our goals, we feel inadequate. The anger, fear, and self-hatred bred by disappointment become the internal basis for the problems we experience in handling life.

When we understand people and their problems within a biblical framework, we can see that there is no mental disorder to be fixed. Rather, there are disturbing internal realities to be faced: the realities of unsatisfied thirst we are determined to quench and of self-protective strategies that we think might do the job. That's what an inside look must expose. When we feel our pain and face our sin, we learn to more richly value the gospel of Christ that provides hope and forgiveness. And, in the process, we find the strength to carry on until we sit down at the banquet table to enjoy the richest of fare.

The overwhelming majority of mail is well represented by one person who wrote to say:

> Reading *Inside Out* was one of the most painful experiences of my life. It opened up a thirst I had never before faced and selfishness I never knew existed within me. But the more I felt my pain and faced my sin, the more valuable grace became. Something has changed deep inside me. I no longer feel hopeless or alone. I'm trusting Christ in ways I never even knew I could. He's becoming more real to me. I feel freer, more alive, less defensive, more willing to wait for heaven's joys than demanding them now, more aware that I want to give to others the hope and acceptance God has given me.

God has used the message of *Inside Out* to stir a deeper appetite for God in hundreds of thousands of people. I'm both surprised and grateful.

But for several years I've had a growing sense that something is missing in the book that I wish were there. One reader put it this way:

> I was deeply helped when I read *Inside Out*. But as I finished the last chapter I found myself thinking it shouldn't have ended. I wanted there to be one more chapter. I'm not certain what I want that chapter to be about, but I think maybe it's joy. When I take an inside look, will I find nothing but disappointed longings and self-protective motives? Isn't there something beneath all the pain and sin in a redeemed heart that, if released, creates a new kind of joy? Just a thought.

A good thought, I've decided. Does inside-out change as I've described it lead merely to getting on better as an empty, sinful person who is persevering till a better day and, in the meantime, trying to sin less? Or does it lead to joy inexpressible? Does the raw experience of disappointment and the admission of selfishness create *joyful* gratitude and hope, or something less?

With these questions stirring in my mind, I read *Inside Out* ten years after writing it and decided to add to the anniversary edition, not only this foreword, but also a new closing chapter I've entitled *The "Good Stuff" Beneath the Bad.*[1]

To the nearly half-million people who have read *Inside Out*, may your journey toward real change continue and be deepened by re-reading the book and its new last chapter. To those who are reading *Inside Out* for the first time, may the reality of joy bubble up from the hidden places in your Spirit-indwelt heart, like springs that send warm water from below to melt the crust of icy snow that keeps the flowers from blooming. May an inside look lead to joyful maturity.

There is joy. There is hope. There is love. There is more in relationship with Christ than we've ever imagined. Press on! He's coming soon! Until then, remember that real change, joyful change, is possible if you're willing to start from the inside out.

NOTES

1. See *Connecting*, a more recent book of mine for further development of this idea (Waco, TX: Word, Inc., 1997).

THE FALSE HOPE OF MODERN CHRISTIANITY

Modern Christianity, in dramatic reversal of its biblical form, promises to relieve the pain of living in a fallen world. The message, whether it's from fundamentalists requiring us to live by a favored set of rules or from charismatics urging a deeper surrender to the Spirit's power, is too often the same: The promise of bliss is for *now!* Complete satisfaction can be ours this side of heaven.

Some speak of the joys of fellowship and obedience, others of a rich awareness of their value and worth. The language may be reassuringly biblical or it may reflect the influence of current psychological thought. Either way, the point of living the Christian life has shifted from knowing and serving Christ till He returns to soothing, or at least learning to ignore, the ache in our soul.

We are told, sometimes explicitly but more often by example, that it's simply not necessary to feel the impact of family tensions, frightening possibilities, or discouraging news. An inexpressible joy is available which, rather than *supporting* us through hard times, can actually *eliminate* pressure, worry, and pain from our experience. Life may have its rough spots, but the reality of *Christ's* presence and blessing can so thrill our soul that pain is virtually unfelt. It simply isn't necessary to wrestle with internal struggle and disorder. Just trust, surrender, persevere, obey.

The effect of such teaching is to blunt the painful reality of what it's like to live as part of an imperfect, and sometimes evil, community. We learn to pretend that we feel now what we cannot feel until heaven.

But not all of us are good at playing the game. Those whose integrity makes such pretense difficult sometimes worry over their apparent lack of faith. "Why don't I feel as happy and together as others? Something must be wrong with my spiritual life." To make matters worse, these people of integrity often appear less mature and their lives less inviting than folks more skilled at denial. And churches tend to reward those members who more convincingly create the illusion of intactness by parading them as examples of what every Christian should be.

Beneath the surface of everyone's life, especially the more mature, is an ache that will not go away. It can be ignored, disguised, mislabeled, or submerged by a torrent of activity, but it will not disappear. And for good reason. We were designed to enjoy a better world than this. And until that better world comes along, we will groan for what we do not have. *An aching soul is evidence not of neurosis or spiritual immaturity, but of realism.*

The experience of groaning, however, is precisely what modern Christianity so often tries to help us escape. The gospel of health and wealth appeals to our legitimate longing for relief by skipping over the call to endure suffering. Faith becomes the means not to learning contentment regardless of circumstances, but rather to rearranging one's circumstances to provide more comfort.

Orthodox Bible preachers rarely are lured into proclaiming a prosperity gospel, but still they appeal to that same desire for relief from groaning. They tell us more knowledge, more commitment, more giving, more prayer—some combination of Christian disciplines—will eliminate our need to struggle with deeply felt realities. Yet there is no escape from an aching soul, only denial of it. The promise of one day being with Jesus in a perfect world is the Christians only hope for complete relief. Until then we either groan or pretend we don't.

The effect of widespread pretense, whether maintained by rigidly living on the surface of life or by being consumed with emotionalism, has been traumatic for the church. Rather than being salt and light, we've become a theologically diverse community of powerless Pharisees, penetrating very little of society because we refuse to grapple honestly with the experience of life.

Beneath much of our claim to orthodoxy, there is a moral cowardice that reflects poorly on our confidence in Christ. We trust Him to forgive our sins and to keep us more or less in line as a community of decent people, but is He enough to deal with things as they really are? Do we know how to face the confusing reality of a world where good parents sometimes have rebellious children and bad parents produce committed missionaries? Can we plunge into the disturbing facts of life and emerge, as the writer of the seventy-third Psalm did, with a renewed confidence in God and a deeper thirst for Him? Can we enter those hidden inner regions of our soul where emptiness is more the reality than a consuming awareness of His presence and where an honest look reveals that self-serving motives stain even our noblest deeds? Is Christ enough to deal with that kind of internal mess? Or is it better never to look at all that and just get on with the Christian life?

When we reflect deeply on how life really is, both inside our soul and outside in our world, a quiet terror threatens to overwhelm us. We worry that we simply won't be able to make it if we face all that is there. In those moments, retreat into denial does not seem cowardly, it seems necessary and smart. Just keep going, get your act together, stop feeling sorry for yourself, renew your commitment to trust God, get more serious about obedience. Things really aren't as bad as you intuitively sense they are. You've simply lost your perspective and must regain it through more time in the Word and increased moral effort.

There is something terribly attractive about knowing what to do to make things better. If we can explain why we feel so bad in terms of something specific and correctable (like not spending enough time in devotions), then we can do something about it. And we like that. Nothing is more terrifying than staring at a problem for which we have no solutions under our direct control. Trusting another is perhaps the most difficult requirement of the

Christian life. We hate to be dependent because we have learned to trust no one, not fully. We know better. Everyone in whom we have placed our confidence has in some way disappointed us. To trust fully, we conclude, is suicide.

Fallen man has taken command of his own life, determined above all else to prove that he's adequate for the job. And like the teen who feels rich until he starts paying for his own car insurance, we remain confident of our ability to manage life until we face the reality of our own soul. Nothing is more humbling than the recognition of (1) a deep thirst that makes us entirely dependent on someone else for satisfaction and (2) a depth of corruption that stains everything we do—even our efforts to reform—with selfishness. To realistically face what is true within us puts us in touch with a level of helplessness we don't care to experience.

A woman admitted to herself that she'd lost all romantic feeling for her kind and thoughtful husband. On the advice of her pastor, she was praying to regain her warmth while at the same time moving toward her husband in chosen obedience. She wanted to believe that the spark was rekindling, but it wasn't. She then tried to convince herself that it didn't matter how she felt; obedience was all that counted. But her lack of romantic feeling for a man who treated her well troubled her deeply. There was nothing she knew to do that could change her internal condition. She felt hopeless.

If awareness of what's inside forces me to admit that I'm utterly dependent on resources outside my control for the kind of change I desire, if helplessness really is at the core of my existence, I prefer to live on the surface of things. It's far more comfortable. To admit I cannot deal with all that's within me strikes a deathblow to my claim to self-sufficiency. To deny the frightening realities within my soul seems as necessary to life as breathing.

It must be said that this state of affairs is thoroughly understandable. We don't like to hurt. And there is no worse pain for fallen people than facing an emptiness we cannot fill. To enter into pain seems rather foolish when we can run from it through denial. We simply cannot get it through our head that, with a nature twisted by sin, the route to joy always involves the very worst sort of internal suffering we can imagine. We rebel at that thought. We weren't designed to hurt. The physical and personal capacities to feel that God built into us were intended to provide pleasures, like good health and close relationships. When they don't, when our head throbs with tension and our heart is broken by rejection, we want relief. With deep passion, we long to experience what we were designed to enjoy.

In the midst of that groaning, the idea that relief may not come is unbearable. It is horrible. How can we continue to live with the ache in our soul provoked by our daughters' abortion or our wife's coldness? How can life go on with a husband who looks for every opportunity to be mean while convinced of his own righteousness? How do we cope with a disfiguring illness, with our guilt over the bitterness we feel as we care for an elderly, helpless parent, with an income that never lets us get ahead?

Into that personal agitation comes the soothing message of modern Christianity: *Relief is available!* Either the disturbing elements in your world will settle down when you develop enough faith, or you can enter a level of spiritual experience in which the struggle to cope is replaced by a fullness of soul. Satisfaction is available, one way or another, and it's available now.

Modern Christianity says it is within our power to arrange for the relief we long for. *We can* learn to claim promises with more faith; *we can* classify sin into manageable categories and then scrupulously avoid it, thereby guaranteeing the blessings we covet; *we can* practice new forms of meditation; *we can* become more involved in church activities and Bible study. It says, *Something we can do will advance us to a level of spirituality that eliminates pain and struggle as ongoing, deeply felt realities.*

The appeal is great. When our soul is thirsty, we can dig our own well. Christian leaders provide the shovels and point out likely spots to dig, and off we go. Discipleship programs, witnessing strategies, Bible memory systems, new forms of community, richer experiences of the Spirit, renewed commitment: the list goes on. Good things to do, but the energy to pursue them is often supplied by the expectation that I'll find water that will end all thirst. No more struggle, disappointment, or heartache. Heaven now.

Not everyone, of course, is teaching this theology. But many are, and many more communicate the same hope by neither sharing honestly their own current struggles nor addressing realistically the struggles of others. It's tempting to stay removed from the problems for which we have no ready answers. It's much easier to preach that we need less counseling and more obedience than to involve ourselves in the messy details of life where obedience comes hard. One result of extricating ourselves from the tangled complexity of life is simplistic preaching that fails to deal with life as it is. Rather than penetrating life with liberating truth, such preaching maintains a conspiracy of pretense that things are better than they are or ever can be until Christ returns. We end up unprepared to live but strengthened in our denial.

A deeply ingrained passion for independence—a legacy left to us by Adam—and a legitimate thirst to enjoy the perfect relationships for which we were designed make us respond eagerly to the hope that heaven's joys are available now—and on demand. When teenagers rebel, hurting parents would love to believe there's a way to replace the terrible heartache with happy confidence. When singleness seems more a prison than an opportunity for expanded service, it would be wonderful to quickly transform the loneliness into a contentment that feels no loss.

Maybe these understandable desires are not within reach. Perhaps the anchor that enables people to weather life's storms and grow through them is gratitude for what happened at the cross of Christ and passionate confidence in what will yet take place at His coming. Could it be that the only source of real stability in the *present* (a kind of stability that does not require the character-weakening mechanism of denial) is appreciation for the *past* and hope for the *future?* Maybe the presence of Christ now, in His Word and Spirit, can be enjoyed only to the degree that it causes us to take both a backward and a forward look.

But such talk seems hopelessly non-immediate, a pie-in-the-sky kind of comfort. We want something *now!* And something is available now, something wonderful and real. But we will find only its counterfeit until we realize that the intensity of our disappointment with life coupled with a Christianity that promises to relieve that disappointment *now* has radically shifted the foundation of our faith. No longer do we resolutely bank everything on the coming of a nail-scarred Christ for His groaning but faithfully waiting people. Our hope has switched to a responsive Christ who satisfies His hurting people by quickly granting them the relief they demand.

That hope, however, is a lie, an appealing but grotesque perversion of the good news of Christ. It's a lie responsible for leading hundreds of thousands of seeking people into either a powerless lifestyle of denial and fabricated joy or a turning away from Christianity in disillusionment and disgust. It's a lie that blocks the path to the deep transformation of character that is available now. We *can* enter into a rich awareness of being alive as a Christian; we *can* taste His goodness in a way that whets our appetite for more. But to demand that our groaning end before heaven keeps us from all that is available now.

God wants to change us into people who are truly noble, people who reflect an unswerving confidence in who He is, which equips us to face all of life and still remain faithful. Spirituality built on pretense is not spirituality at all. God wants us to be courageous people who are deeply bothered by the horrors of living as part of a fallen race, people who look honestly at every struggle, who feel overwhelmed by what we see, yet emerge prepared to live: scarred, still troubled, but deeply loving. When the fact is faced that life is profoundly disappointing, the only way to make it is to learn to love. And only those who are no longer consumed with finding satisfaction *now* are able to love. Only when we commit our yearnings for perfect joy to a Father we have learned to deeply trust are we free to live for others despite the reality of a perpetual ache.

This book is not about relief; it is about change. Its message is not, "Here's how to feel better now." Rather, it deals with the route to transformation of character.

That route, it should be noted, takes a surprising twist that cannot be seen from the narrow gate leading into it. After traveling the route for some time (one never knows how much time, but certainly more than those who are committed to immediate relief would ever endure), something unexpected and wonderful occurs. A hint of one's substance develops and a glimpse of what it means to be *alive* awakens the soul to its unrealized potential for joy. And that glimpse so clearly reflects the beauty of Christ's involvement with us that a self-sufficient pride in one's value becomes unthinkable.

The ache remains, and even intensifies, as more of the fallen reality of our own soul is exposed. But the notion that our present suffering is nothing in comparison with the glory ahead begins to make sense.

I'm not very far along the path to deeply felt life and joy in Christ, but I think I'm on it. Consider with me what is available in this life: a change of character that enables us to taste enough of God now to whet our appetite for the banquet later.

The kind of internal change that permits a richer taste of God is possible, but it requires surgery. The disease blocking our enjoyment of God has spread beyond the point where more effort to do what we think is right will be enough. And there is no anesthetic as the knife penetrates our soul.

But this kind of change—change from the inside out—is worth the pain. It makes the Christian life possible. It frees us to groan without complaint, to love others in spite of our emptiness, and to wait for the complete satisfaction we so desperately desire.

PART ONE
LOOKING BENEATH THE SURFACE OF LIFE

"Don't look inside me—I'm not sure I like what's there."

CHAPTER ONE

REAL CHANGE REQUIRES AN INSIDE LOOK

Although this book is written to anyone who wants to better understand how we can really change, certain groups of people come to mind as I write. First, *those who are trying hard to do what the Bible commands but feel frustrated.* You are doing all you know to do—not perfectly of course, but sincerely. And yet things just aren't right inside, and you know it. You feel more pressure than joy. God isn't changing either you or things in your world the way you ask Him to. You wonder if He listens to your prayers or if He simply doesn't care about your struggles.

Worries over money or children, hurt caused by a friend or spouse, fears about whether you can handle whatever problems may arise tomorrow—all keep you awake at night. Tears are for the night, the Bible says, but joy comes in the morning (Psalm 30:5). But the sunrise brings no relief for you, just more pressure. You don't know what else to do to find those green pastures and still waters. You plug along but with a weight on your back that keeps you feeling heavy.

My message to you is, *There's hope!* More effort isn't the answer. Continued obedience is required, of course, but looking for more hoops to jump through before God becomes real is not the way.

Freedom and quiet rest can replace the pressure and churning in your soul. But finding peace requires an honest look into your life at some hard things. Jumping through more hoops is sometimes easier than facing troubling things inside. But an inside look can lead to real change, change from the inside out.

Second, I think of *those who are doing quite well and feel content and happy most of the time.* You really do love the Lord, you have proved Him real and faithful in hard times. Time in His Word is often a rich experience. Prayer is far more than mere ritual in your life. You like your church, you're blessed with good friends and family, you feel satisfied with your work, and you enjoy your leisure time. Your life is not without tensions, but God gives you the strength to press on with confidence. By the grace of God, life is good.

My message to you is, *There's more!* Gratefully enjoy the blessings of God and live out the maturity He has developed in you— but don't settle for it. Don't let your legitimate comfort become complacency or your joy slip into smugness. There is more to knowing God than the most mature Christian has ever envisioned. Be willing to have the steadiness in your life disrupted if knowing God better requires it. The good fight is fought with a sweaty passion that develops only when the evenness of our soul is upset. God wants to change good disciples into powerfully loving servants who leave an indelible mark on people they touch. But His method of changing us, from the inside out, can be disturbing. Be open to new levels of struggle.

Third, I think of *those who are hardened.* Nothing has really gone your way. The promises of God you were taught don't seem to materialize, at least not in *your* life. Perhaps you've always felt different, never a good fit like your brother or sister. Youth leaders never considered your name for "boy or girl of the year" in your church. Your parents never held you up as the model for other kids to follow.

Teenage years (perhaps you're still there) were rough. You indulged in some drinking and drugs (more than your parents ever suspected) and sexual activity beyond moral boundaries. You made promises to God to reform that lasted a week after youth camp ended. You feel discouraged, hard. You attend church.

Perhaps others are convinced that you're a nice normal Christian; you know how to play the game. But inside you're angry, cold, scared. Why "try God" again? It never worked before.

My message to you is, *There's life!* Pat answers won't do and you know it. Commitments to read your Bible every day and keep a spiritual journal may be good medicine for a lesser disease, but it won't work for you. Promises to make better friends, to spend more time in church, are not the paths to life. You've tried it. Maybe there is no life for you, just continued pretending with the occasional relief of "worldly pleasures."

If you're willing to be honest about some private matters that people rarely look at, to face some things about your life beneath the indifference and hardness, then talk about an abundant life can become more than irritating rhetoric. Meaning, relationships that stir you to joy and a sense of quiet wholeness as you face life are all available. But not easily and not overnight. The route is uphill, but you can change from the inside out.

Fourth, I think of *those who are in positions of Christian leadership.* The pressure to model for others what maturity looks like can lead to breakdown or pride. You realize that others think of you as better than you know yourself to be. It's hard to maintain an image. But the pressure to encourage people by displaying what God can do in a life surrendered to Him makes you hide a few of the real struggles.

Some of you are rightly grateful for the maturity that years of commitment have yielded. But you know the line between gratitude and pride is thin. Some of you are tired, close to burnout, weary of the loneliness that comes from battling with temptations you feel free to share with no one.

My message to you is, *There's love!* The church needs leaders who can involve themselves in other people's lives with the joy of integrity and transparency, confident that their love is unfeigned, willing to be deeply known for the sake of helping others. That awful distance from people that the aura of leadership creates can be bridged. The struggles that sometimes tear at your soul can be dealt with. Vulnerability, humility, intimacy, power—qualities of character that the pressures of leadership often weaken—can be developed. The model of a loving servant that our Lord both illustrated and taught can be followed. But more is required than keeping your head above the water of expectations and responsibilities. A long hard look at your life, preferably with a trusted friend, may be necessary to slow down the hectic pace of a life committed to ministry and to identify those internal issues buried beneath the demands of leadership. The joys of influence are available to people who change from the inside out.

Perhaps you don't easily fit into any of these groups. But you do bear Gods image; you were built to resemble God. The message of Christianity is that a relationship with Christ is available that can reach into every part of your life and can move you toward becoming the person He saved you to be. Real change is possible!

Be patient as you read this book. Some of what I say will be unclear at points and may seem more relevant to others than to you. I urge you to read on. When we get down to the bottom line of who we are and what struggles we experience, we're all pretty much alike: We long for a life that's real and full and happy, and we all think we can make this kind of life happen.

Our Lord came to bring life. We can possess His life now and look forward to enjoying perfect life later. Between the time when He gives us life and the time when He provides all the joys His life brings, He intends to change us into people who can more deeply enjoy Him now and represent Him well to others. The surgery required to make that change is always painful. But God will settle for nothing less than deep change in our character, a radical transformation and restructuring of how we approach life. This book is about that kind of change, change that flows from the inside out.

What Does It Mean to Change?

A good friend of mine recently sat in my office thinking out loud about whatever came to mind. The topics ranged from his marriage (which had its share of disappointments), to his future plans for ministry, to the quality of his walk with the Lord. As the conversation continued his mood became increasingly thoughtful—

not gloomy, but quietly and deeply reflective, the kind of mood no one ever feels in a fast-food restaurant.

My friend, I should point out, is a committed Christian, a gifted counselor, and an unusually clear thinker. His life has known a few trials, but nothing remarkably different from what most middle-aged men have experienced. His friends describe him as friendly, hardworking, loyal, and sincere. A few see his spontaneous fun-loving side. Everyone agrees he's a solid, well-adjusted Christian.

After nearly an hour of reflective rambling, his thoughtful mood shifted into a profoundly sad, almost desperate, loneliness. As though talking to no one in particular, he quietly said, "I wonder what it would be like to feel really good for just ten minutes."

His sentence struck me. Did I know what it was like to feel really good for ten minutes? A fair number of people look reasonably happy. Do they feel really good? Utterly happy with no hint of emptiness or sorrow?

Maybe the question is wrong. Perhaps Christians are supposed to ask, "Do I know what it means to be consistently obedient?" and not worry about their feelings. But then, what is Peter referring to when he speaks of inexpressible joy (1 Peter 1:8)?

What is a maturing Christian like on the inside? What will he feel? Will he have a consistent desire to do what's right? Or will he fight a raging battle within between urges to do wrong and commitments to do right?

Does maturity feel good? Or is there a deepened sense of loneliness and struggle? Will there be the awareness of a thoroughly changed set of motives that delights to do God's will? Or will there continue to be evidence of corruption within? Will the pursuit of holiness lead to an increase in happiness? As we grow stronger, do we *feel* stronger—or weaker?

Some people honestly feel quite happy. Are they pretending? Should they be struggling more? When others show deep pain and overwhelming frustration, these folks can't relate to them any more than someone well fed can feel the horror of starvation. Perhaps these "happy" people's lives reflect a healthy stability and contentment that we could wish for everyone. What does it mean for these folks to press on toward higher levels of maturity?

What does it mean to change, to grow, to conform more and more to the image of Christ? What kind of change is possible, and how does it come about?

The Appearance of Maturity: Looking Good

Not long ago I spoke to a large group of Christian leaders, men and women who had distinguished themselves in both business and church circles. The setting was a large, comfortable auditorium with thickly cushioned, theater-style seats. The mood was pleasant and cordial. People looked happy. Their appropriately fashionable clothing and the social ease with which they mingled before the meeting suggested that, unlike my friend, they felt really good. There was no evidence of struggle. Things looked fine, much as they do on a Sunday morning in church, where people chat warmly in the hallways and sit attentively during the service.

Sometimes when I stand before a group of such together-looking people, I feel a bit intimidated. I study the sea of faces before me and wonder: Am I the only one who feels a nagging sense that something is badly twisted within me? Is no one else struggling with the quality of their relationships, aware that despite their best efforts the depth of their love is still pretty shallow? Does no one else feel like a failure, at least occasionally?

Perhaps I'm an obsessive perfectionist who has yet to learn how to relax, to take life as it comes, appreciating the good and accepting the bad. Maybe people healthier than I have come to depend on God in a way that permits a more balanced life with less internal confusion and struggle. Yet as I looked out on the group I was about to address, I knew some were struggling with significant trials. In any large group, including an impressive collection of respected and successful people like the group I was addressing, there are, of course, some whose lives are breaking apart under the weight of financial pressures, health problems, rebellious teens, and strained marriages.

In the front row sat a missionary friend of mine who had just completed twenty-five years of faithful service in a difficult situation. Earlier that week he'd confided in me, choking back tears as he spoke, that his marriage was full of tension and he had no idea how to move closer to his wife. His teenage sons were adjusting to life in America by listening to rock music, and he wasn't sure whether to put an end to it or to say nothing. He told me he felt like a failure, able to do missionary work but incompetent to lead his own family. I was certain he wasn't the only one in the audience struggling with hard things.

But even among the strugglers there were undoubtedly a fair number who were sailing through their trials with an evenness and stability I could only envy. I've been with people when they heard news that would have shattered me. And their response was to thank God for His faithfulness, pray for strength, and press on.

Was that real? Do people like that not feel the crushing weight of bad news as a heaviness that sometimes robs them of a desire to go on? Do they not wrestle with their own ability to handle tough decisions? Are they as calm and confident as they appear?

Certainly there are those whose problems get the best of them, people who seek escape in drinking or drugs or spending or sex, others whose internal tensions find expression in depressed feelings or anxiety attacks or thoughts of suicide. These folks, most agree, need special help to get back on track. But the other people, those who even on close inspection seem to be doing well, are the ones who disturb me. They look so together. Have they really found a way to live that keeps them calm and happy and motivated to do right? Some, I think, have.

But I wonder if most people who look good all the time are really out of touch with themselves, unaware of how they impact others, and covering up deep pain with the pleasures of activity and achievement. Perhaps much of what passes for spiritual maturity is maintained by a rigid denial of all that is happening beneath the surface of their lives. Maybe in this life it's impossible to be as together as some people look.

The Way Things Are Beneath the Appearance

No matter how together we may appear, even to ourselves, buried deep within our heart is the vague sense that something is wrong, dreadfully wrong. We feel a twinge of discomfort when someone puts us on the spot; we sense a pressure to play it safe when a friend's tone becomes critical; we well up with anger when a spouse misunderstands us, we're aware of shifting conversation to a topic we can handle; we look for opportunities to modestly share some information that makes us look good; we pretend to be more spiritually minded than we actually are; we avoid subjects that put us in touch with unpleasant emotions.

Just a quick glance beneath the surface of our life makes it clear that more is going on than loving God and loving others. It requires only a moment of honest self-reflection to realize that, no matter how much we may have already changed, we still have a long way to go. Most of us know things about ourselves that no one else would guess: thoughts, fantasies, things we do in private, secrets that make us feel ashamed. We know things are not as they should be. Something is wrong.

Ever since God expelled Adam and Eve from the garden, we have lived in an unnatural environment, a world in which we were not designed to live. We were built to enjoy a garden without weeds, relationships without friction, fellowship without distance. But something is wrong, and we know it, both within our world and within ourselves. Deep inside we sense we're out of the nest, always ending the day in a motel room, never at home. When we're honest, we see we handle our discomfort by keeping our distance from people, responding more to our fears than to another's desire for love.

We wish we were better than we are, but we're not. And that realization brings shame, a desire to hide, to avoid real contact, to present to others only that part of us we think will be well received. We want to hide the rest—not because we desire to avoid offending others with our ugly side, but because we fear their rejection. We live for the purpose of self-protection, clinging to whatever brings us happiness and security. The effect is a discouraging distance between ourselves and the people we long to be close to. The quality of our life diminishes.

Unlike the proverbial alligator under the bed, our problem is real. The little children who sometimes keep their hands away from the sides of their beds to prevent the alligator crawling on the floor from biting them off are genuinely afraid, but their fears are entirely unfounded. There is no alligator in the bedroom. But there really is something wrong in our world. Reality is not as we want it to be. We sense that something is badly twisted within us and in our world because it is. Our longing to feel really good is not always neurotic discontent; it may be legitimate. We desire what we do not have and cannot have until Christ returns and restores everything, including ourselves, to the way it was meant to be. Until then, that intuitive awareness of trouble that clouds our happiest moments is reflecting not the fear of an imaginary alligator but a basic truth about life in a fallen world.

Most of us spend our life trying to pretend things are better than they are. When reality breaks through—perhaps in a glimpse of how disappointed or imperfect we are—we're strongly inclined to do whatever restores our feigned sense of well-being. We may count our blessings, cut the lawn, pray for strength, eat something sweet, consult a counselor, join the church choir, fight with our spouse, read a favorite psalm, turn on the TV, scold ourselves for being a downer, re-surrender ourselves to God, or go out with friends for pizza—anything to get away from that nagging sense that something is missing, something is wrong. Most of us are not consciously aware of trying to get rid of personal discomfort by eating pizza. We just happen to like pizza. But perhaps more often than we know, the things we do are designed to bring relief from a vague sense of emptiness we may hardly notice.

Maybe my friend who wondered what ten minutes of pure good feelings would be like was touching that painful reality of wanting to be home but always living in a motel. Maybe he was more honestly aware of how things really are than the together people, most of whom would express concern for someone as gloomy as my friend.

Perhaps the majority of people who report pleasant feelings with only occasional struggles are building their houses on sand by preserving their happiness through pretense; or, to change the image, maybe they're rearranging the furniture in the motel room, hoping it will feel like home. When we succeed at arranging our life so that "all is well," we keep ourselves from facing all that's going on inside. And when we ignore what's happening on the inside, we lose all power to change what we do on the outside in any meaningful way. We *rearrange* rather than *change,* and in so doing, we never become the transformed person God calls us to be. We never experience freedom from destructive patterns of living.

In this book, I want to explore what it means to change. How can a woman who was molested as a child enter joyfully into sexual union with her husband? How can a man who feels easily threatened become a strong leader in his home? How can well-adjusted people whose lives are working reasonably well become rich people whose firsthand knowledge of God draws others to Him? How can parents go on with their lives when their kids are moving in terrible directions? How can we change into noble people whose source of strength and joy is in finding our home in Christ?

I am not primarily concerned in this book to look at specific problems we face, but rather to study a few basic ideas that underlie all biblical efforts to change. Most of us make it through life by coping, not changing. We rearrange what we do, but somehow the core problems involving who we really are remain only partially addressed.

Change as our Lord describes it involves more than cleaning up our visible act. He intends us to do more than sweep the streets; He wants us to climb down into the sewers and do something about the filth beneath the concrete. He directs us to enter the dark regions of our soul to find light, to experience His presence when we feel most alone. Biblical change never requires us to pretend that things are better than they are. Christ wants us to face reality as it is, including all the fears, hurts, resentments, and self-protective motives we work hard to keep out of sight, and to emerge as changed people. Not pretenders. Not perfect. But more able to deeply love because we're more aware of His love.

Can I Make It If I Face It?

Perhaps the most frequently expressed fear people feel when they begin to look closely at their lives is this: "I'm not sure I can make it if I face all that's inside me." It requires courage to explore our

life honestly. There really is an alligator. Our fears have substance.
In fact, a clear awareness of even a small part of how lonely and
self-serving we really are is overwhelming. Every new insight into
our soul feels like one more nail in our coffin.[1] How people really
feel about us, what our motives are as we interact with a colleague
or tell jokes at a party, how disappointed and angry we are with our
parents or spouse or children—the list is long.

Most of us make it through life with some level of stability
because we refuse to think about troubling things going on within
us. We just keep on keeping on, stifling that nagging sense that
something's wrong, that there has to be more. We want to think
we've found the key to life, that now we can manage, that our
empty heart is filled, that our struggle against sin is now a march
of victory. But in order to maintain that happy conviction we must
insulate ourselves against the feedback of others who find us still
unloving, and we must stubbornly deny the evidence in our soul
that more is wrong than we know how to handle. Denial for many
becomes a way of life. And years of practice make it possible to
seal off from our awareness any data that contradicts what we want
to believe. It's frighteningly easy to become deluded about our spiritual maturity.

Hosea scorned the Jews of his day for having heads sprinkled
with gray hair and not knowing it (Hosea 7:9). Normally, we're
the first to spot evidence of physical decline and aging, such as
gray hair. But just as normally, we're the last to notice signs of spiritual deterioration. And that's Hosea's point. We're capable of believing we're doing far better than we are.

Our Lord reserved His harshest criticism for people who made
denial into a trademark. The Pharisees specialized in looking
good. They managed to preserve their image by defining sin in
terms of visible transgressions and then scrupulously adhering to
the standards they established. Their source of joy was the respect
of others, and they found effective means of gaining it. They
performed well. Their level of disciplined conformity to external
expectations was high. I suspect very few of their numbers would
have reported a longing to feel good for just ten minutes. These
were the together people.

Had I been invited to address one of their meetings, I think I would have felt more than a little intimidated. They didn't seem to be struggling. They'd found what they were after and were proceeding confidently with an enviable degree of personal adjustment. These people looked good.

But listen to our Lord's remarks when He spoke to them. They impressed others, but not Him.

> "Woe to you, teachers of the law and Pharisees, you hypocrites! You clean the outside of the cup and dish, but inside they are full of greed and self-indulgence. Blind Pharisee! First clean the inside of the cup and dish, and then the outside also will be clean." (Matthew 23:25-26)

He went on to make the unfavorable comparison between their lives and attractively whitewashed gravestones, telling them that a look beneath the surface of their outwardly righteous behavior would reveal the stench of decay and corruption, just as removal of the gravestone would expose the rotting flesh of dead bodies. Small wonder He wasn't a favorite speaker at their conventions.

In His rebuke to the Pharisees, our Lord declared a principle that must guide all our efforts to change into the person God wants us to be. He made it clear that there is no place for pretense. We must come to grips with what's going on behind the whitewashed appearance of our life. It seems to be His teaching that we can't make it if we don't face all that we are. To look honestly at those parts of our experience we naturally deny is painful business, so painful that the analogy of death is not too strong. But to change according to Christ's instructions requires us to face all we prefer to deny. *Real change requires an inside look.*

Shallow Copers Versus Troubled Reflecters

People tend to fall into one of two categories: (1) those who successfully ignore the inward ache and corruption and get on, more or less effectively, with life; and (2) those who, for whatever reason, are gripped by an awareness that something is terribly wrong and, as a result, struggle in their efforts to move along through life.

The great majority of Christians, myself included, would much rather enjoy whatever is pleasant, do what we should, and learn to endure whatever trials may come our way. Growth for most sincere Christians means continued effort to do all we should as we avail ourselves of whatever means of enablement we believe God has provided. Some seek a fuller experience of God's Spirit. Others try to get to a point of decisive surrender. Still others try to find the help to live as they should through prayer, fellowship, and learning God's Word. The focus in all these approaches is to do what God commands with God's help. And that focus is, of course, right and proper. There is no growth without a commitment to follow Christ and to live in dependence upon Him for the power to do so. The priorities of obedience and dependence are essential to real change.

But a focus on the responsibility to obey and to appropriate God's power sometimes leads us away from the regions of our life that present the greatest challenges. We work at cleaning up our outside, sometimes feeling an almost unbearable pressure to change as we should. Like the Pharisees, we reduce sin to manageable categories and expend all our energies in maintaining the standards we set. Spirituality then comes to be measured by not attending movies and never missing church rather than by an improvement in the quality of our relationships. The hard-to-handle issues in our soul that keep us from relating to others deeply and constructively are ignored; and easier-to-handle matters, such as social courtesies and appropriate language, become widely accepted barometers of spiritual health.

When this focus on measurable, superficial behavior serves to divert attention away from troubling realities within our soul, as it often does, then its effect is to help us cope by conforming our behavior to whatever standards we set. Change is largely external. It's not from the inside out. And its effect is to increase a deep sense of pressure, not freedom.

Call this first group *shallow copers,* people who cope with life by dealing with whatever they can handle and ignoring all the rest.

Among these folks, the priority of the pulpit may reduce fellowship to mere activity and tough accountability. Rich encouragement and stirring love may be lost. Discipleship sometimes becomes only an opportunity for more teaching rather than an honest grappling with the real problems of life. Looking deeply into one's heart is discouraged as unnecessary and self-absorbing.

A second group of people have difficulty adjusting in a community of shallow copers. They cannot rid themselves of the gnawing awareness that more is wrong than renewed efforts at obedience seem to correct. Call these people *troubled reflecters,* folks who wrestle honestly with at least some of the disturbing parts of their lives for which they have no real answers.

The route to real change is more often found by people who realistically face difficulties than by those who manage to preserve pleasant feelings by ignoring the tough things in their lives. An honest look at problems creates struggles that have more hope of leading to deep change than does a complacency supported by denial.

Shallow copers may become troubled reflecters when something traumatic happens to upset their confidence in their ability to handle life, like a daughter developing anorexia, a spouse deserting the family, or a son retreating into rebellious anger. Even then, they tend to search for some way to cope without ever looking honestly at the issues in their own hearts and at the quality of their relationships. "Yes, it's true that my son is far from the Lord. We've done everything we know to do, but for now Satan is getting the upper hand. We're just committing him to the Lord, praying in faith that God will bring him back soon." Case closed. The effort to cope with life is not only shallow, it has now become rigid. Any suggestion that more could be looked at, including the possibility that the son may never return or that Dad may have angrily demanded a high level of obedience less for his son's sake than for his own, is regarded as a violation of trusting the Lord.

Too often, a commitment to obedience reflects not a passionate desire to pursue God, but a stubbornly fearful determination to not feel deep frustration and personal pain. When the energy behind our obedience is supplied by the desire to deny pain, the warm, fleshy parts of the human soul are not engaged in following God. We become stiff. Dogmatism, a demand that we indoctrinate others with our understanding of what is moral, replaces an openness to investigating what God might really want from us. We lose touch with the throbbing reality of honest communication with people. We become rigid moralists who push people to keep God's standards rather than passionate Christians who entice others to know Christ better.

Comforting thoughts about God's faithfulness can keep us living on the surface of life, safely removed from a level of pain and confusion that seems overwhelming. But God is most fully known in the midst of confusing reality. To avoid asking the tough questions and facing the hard issues is to miss a transforming encounter with God.

Change Requires an Inside Look

More and more people are having trouble maintaining a comfortable adjustment based on denial. Life is just too confusing, relationships too difficult, experiences too disappointing, and responsibilities too burdensome for people to easily pretend that the keys to effective living are just doing their duty and denying all that troubles them.

Parents are finding little help in all the popular formulas and principles as they try to deal with their daughter who is lying to them more and more. They no longer feel confident as they do all they know to do. Too many other kids from good homes have gone bad to permit a happy confidence that everything will turn out well.

Women are admitting to themselves that their womanhood is more a neutral fact than a unique source of joy. And beneath that dull neutrality, more women are recognizing a deep fear of being hurt that keeps them from enjoying their opportunities to give of themselves.

Men sense their weakness and wish with all their hearts that they knew how to be meaningfully involved with their families. But their efforts to lovingly lead end up in failure. They then retreat to whatever sphere of life offers them a sense of competence, and live without the rich joy of being involved husbands and fathers.

Christians are realizing that their version of church involvement, time in the Word, commitment to do right, claiming God's promises, and surrendering to God's power is somehow not getting at the core troubles of their hearts.

We want more, and are therefore vulnerable to following anyone who convincingly holds out the promise of more. We try the latest spiritual fad, we attend the currently popular seminar or crusade, we listen diligently to the tapes of our favorite preacher—and we always come up short. Nothing satisfies, nothing works. In our heart, we know that our latest effort to follow Christ has left deep issues in our soul unaddressed.

Is it possible to change at the core of our being? How much change can we expect? The disturbing reality within us, which we try to pretend isn't there, makes us wonder just how changed we can become.

This book is about changing from the inside out, a process that begins with an honest look at whatever is happening in our life and continues without ever pretending things are better than they are. The courage to be honest is necessary if we're to experience the kind of change our Lord makes possible. Real change requires an inside look.

NOTES

1. I must anticipate later discussion by mentioning now that the lethal blow is dealt not to our humanity, but to its corruption. Because our soul is so thoroughly stained with self-reliance, the death of pride feels like the death of our self. However, the more terrible the blow to our efforts to preserve our own life, to arrange it so we experience the minimum amount of pain, the more we emerge as truly alive. The process seems confusing only because it cuts across all our ideas about how to live.

CHAPTER TWO

AN INSIDE LOOK CAN BE FRUSTRATING

I remember sitting in Sunday school as a small boy, listening attentively to my teacher describing the Christian's struggle to be good. He said that within each of us there is a *bad dog* and a *good dog*. The bad dog, we were told, could never be tamed into a lovable pet. The good dog, however, was placed in our heart by God when we became a Christian and it was already tame. It always wanted to do the right thing.

The bad dog was our old nature, that part of our insides that reliably urges us to do wrong. The good dog, our new nature, could always whip the bad dog in a fight, but it would never spring into action *unless told to do so*. And that was the key. Whenever we felt tempted to glance at the smart kid's spelling paper during a test, that was the bad dog barking. At that moment, the Christian's job was to say "sic 'em" to the good dog—and we would keep our eyes where they belonged.

The teacher went on to gravely warn us that the bad dog could never be killed, not until we reached heaven. He taught us what I have subsequently heard repeated in countless sermons: although we were saved from the *penalty* and *power* of sin, we are not delivered from the *presence* of sin until the next life. Our sinful nature always manages to recover from its wounds to prod us again in wrong directions. Our only hope is to learn to say "sic 'em" to the good dog for the rest of our life. To the degree we do so, we can enjoy a life of consistent victory over sin and joyful fellowship with God.

I recall listening to this teaching and feeling confused. "But how do you say 'sic 'em' to the good dog?" I wondered. "I'm not sure exactly what I'm supposed to do."

The metaphor was graphic and it seemed to square with the biblical idea about two opposing forces waging war within us, but I couldn't make the whole thing work during a spelling test. When I managed to *not* look at my neighbor's paper, it seemed to me that I'd simply chosen, for whatever reason, to do the right thing. I couldn't see that the power of God was involved at all. I had made a choice, the same way a moral nonChristian would. And when I felt myself about to cheat, issuing commands to some mythical dog failed to help. I either gave in or I resisted, depending on the force of the temptation and a host of other factors—none of which had any apparent relationship to the interaction of God's power with my internal processes. I really wanted to be good, but my early teaching provided more frustration than clear guidance. An inside look wasn't helpful. Making choices seemed to be the only issue, so I tried hard to make good choices.

Today, when I listen to sermons and read books on how to become the person I should be—joyful, self-sacrificing, dedicated, humble, uncompromising, loving—I often get that same feeling. I sense (with a confidence I can't always defend) that there is a path to becoming the person Christ wants me to be and that means for walking that path are available. But I'm frequently unsure of how to piece it all together, other than to simply choose to obey.

Doing Good Versus Being Good

Some people reflect one or perhaps several of the characteristics I want to see in me, but no one (except our Lord) presents me with a complete picture of all I want to be. That observation tells me that at any stage of my spiritual development I will be, at best, a flawed representation of what a Christian should look like. I cannot be perfect—but I can be better. I can be more like our Lord and more like those followers of His who've incorporated a few facets of His beauty in their makeup.

The kind of improvement I really long for, however, goes much deeper than an external likeness. I can name scores of people who evidence *patterns of behavior* I would do well to emulate. But the list is far shorter of people whose *character qualities* I admire. Lots of people are industrious, disciplined, knowledgeable, even hospitable. And those things are good. But only a few people seem truly giving, compassionate, or noble. I *respect* the more superficial of these worthwhile characteristics, but I *admire* the deeper qualities, those that indicate significant character change.

Let me clarify what I mean—the point is important. One friend comes to mind who is self-disciplined in his health habits. He resists temptation to eat too many sweets, he jogs faithfully, and he paces his workload well. I respect him for that. His behavior reflects a commendable level of willpower, a level that sometimes puts to shame my efforts to eat, exercise, and work properly.

Another friend responds to a terribly disappointing and painful struggle in his life by loving others more deeply. He feels his pain but somehow uses it to make himself more aware of others pain and of God's ability to encourage. When I look at his life, words like noble, godly, and rich come to mind.

Observing habits of self-discipline, orderliness, and general cordiality do not bring to mind those same words. I describe my well-disciplined friend as effective, respectable, and nice. When I look at his life I think, "I should be more disciplined." I feel a bit pressured, somewhat guilty, and occasionally motivated. The effect of my struggling friend, on the other hand, is *not* to make me say, "I *should* be more disciplined," but "I *want* to be more loving."

The difference is enormous. Some people push me to *do* better by trying harder. Others draw me to *be* better by enticing me with an indefinable quality about their lives that seems to grow out of an unusual relationship with Christ, one that really means something, one that goes beyond correct doctrine and appropriate dedication to personally felt reality. The few who report occasional glimpses of Christ that touch their souls more deeply than any other experience of life are the ones who excite me with the possibility of change. I want to be a different *kind* of person, not just someone whose behavior patterns and biblical knowledge are commendable. To change who I am requires a very different process than the process needed to change what I do or what I know. Cosmetic surgery is not adequate for the kind of change I have in mind.

I want to do more than exercise kindness toward my wife; I want to freely give to her from deep resources within me. I want to do more than teach my kids what's expected and then enforce rules to keep them in line; I want to draw them by my life into the pursuit of God. I want to do more than preach sermons that are biblically sound, well delivered, and warmly received; I want to pour out my soul in ways that convey truth with personal power. I want to do more than control my tendency toward depression; I want to taste the goodness of God to such an extent that I'm confident of perfect joy ahead.

This kind of change calls for more than dedicated effort on my part can produce. I'm talking about change in the very depths of my being, change of which I have less a taste than a vision, change I see little of in many, a great deal of in few, and fully manifested in only One. I want this kind of change, but when people try to describe how to achieve it, I feel frustrated.

Suppose my Sunday school teacher would simply have said, "Look, I know you are tempted to cheat in school. It's wrong, you might get caught, and giving in could lead to patterns that may foul up your life later. So don't do it. Make a decision to keep your eyes on your own paper and then try your hardest to keep them there. It will be tough and you'll fail sometimes. When you do, ask God to forgive you and go back to trying hard to not do it again." That lesson would have made sense to me, much more than his talk about two dogs growling inside. It's when people talk about what's required for *inside* change that I get confused. I understand moral effort, but good patterns of behavior alone, no matter how intense or strenuous, cannot produce those deeper character qualities I admire and properly covet.

Performance or Dependence?

For centuries Christians have grappled with how we are to work out our own salvation (which seems to involve real effort) while somehow depending on God to work inside us, enabling us by His strength to desire and carry out His will. If we are to be more than humanistic, relying on our own resources to become all we can be, then *dependence on God* as we seek to obey Him must go beyond inspiring rhetoric. It must become vital reality.

But just how do we depend completely on God? The answer is elusive (simple, I think, as I hope later chapters will show, but still elusive). And because it's elusive, most modern approaches to understanding ourselves and changing come back to the central ingredient of effort. Whether our problem is doing something we wish we weren't doing or wanting to completely surrender ourselves to God or struggling to believe we really are loved by God, the bottom line is still the same: *Try harder!*

The strategy for change based on effort is more easily defined than is the one rooted in dependence on God. For that reason, I suspect sermons usually involve instruction about the Bible's content, followed by exhortations to live consistently with it. Knowledge and obedience. Learn more and do right. But the product of a life committed only to gaining knowledge and living properly is that first kind of character quality: the ones that command respect but fail to draw us more deeply into relationship.

Our Lord made it clear that doing right in His eyes required far more than the performance of certain activities. The entire law, He said, could be summarized in two commands: Love God and love others. We cannot honor these exhortations in even the smallest measure without profound internal change. Moral effort alone can never produce genuine love.

I believe it can be successfully argued that every personal or behavioral problem one might wish to change (for example, bad temper, perverted sexual desires, depression, anxiety, overeating) results ultimately from violations of the command to love. If that's true, then learning to love is not only necessary for spiritual maturity, but also central to overcoming psychological problems. When we're convinced that every problem in living, both between people and within them, reflects a style of relating that violates God's standards of love, and when we see that learning to love is an inside job requiring far more than moral effort, we will be eager to take an inside look.

But now we're back where we started. Once we grant that we must poke our head beneath the surface of our life if we are to really change, we're faced with the considerable dilemma of figuring out our own insides and exactly what we're supposed to do with them. Where do we begin?

Dealing with Life Below the Waterline

Think of yourself as an iceberg. Let the visible peak above the waterline represent the things you do, the thoughts you consciously think, and the feelings you sense within you. Let the great mass beneath the waterline represent the part of you that cannot be clearly seen: the motives and attitudes of your heart, those strange impulses that sometimes overwhelm your determination to resist them, the painful memories and raging emotions you prefer to keep hidden beneath the surface of your life.

We know that handling the part of us that's above the waterline requires effort. We must choose to do right. We must study to think right. We must control the expression of our emotions without losing our spontaneity. But the effort to do right, think right, and control our emotions leads quickly to frustration. If our standards remain high, we must admit that more is going on inside us than extra effort can handle. The question then becomes: What are we to do with the part of us that is beneath the waterline, those elements that do not change through stronger attempts to do right? We might sketch it as shown on the following page.

The Christian community generally presents three options for dealing with the confusing realities beneath the waterline. All three

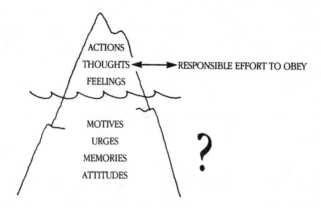

promise deep internal change. In the rest of this chapter, I want to briefly outline these options, each of which has value but is incomplete and unnecessarily frustrating.

Option 1: Do Your Christian Duties

Perhaps the most common understanding of how change comes about is this: If we determine to do whatever God says, and if we couple that determination with involvement in Christian activities, then somehow the power of God is released, enabling us to live as we should.

We're told we must obey God but that we must do it in His strength. Every effort to live in the power of the flesh will inevitably fail. Above the waterline, we do what we should, including immersing ourselves in God's Word, praying, and serving others. As we do these things, God's power eventually overwhelms all those problems below the waterline and we are enabled to live in consistent victory.

When we fail above the waterline, then more effort is called for—perhaps spending more time in the Word or in prayer or enlisting in our church's witnessing campaign. Obedience to Christian duty and bathing our mind and soul in God's truth keep us from quenching or grieving the Holy Spirit. As we free Him to work powerfully in our life, His grace enables us to do what's right. There is no need for an inside look. Whatever issues are rumbling beneath the surface will sort themselves out as God gets hold of our life through the performance of Christian duties. An inside look seems to be an unnecessary and damaging psychological side-track on the path to maturity.

So many have come to me for professional counseling after years of doing their Christian duties without experiencing the expected benefit. They wonder what went wrong. Rising earlier for devotions simply has not helped; they're tired, discouraged, disillusioned. Others I've known have spent years in Bible study, prayer, and church activity and, as a result, have become rigid, well-disciplined, distant Christians who do right and relate poorly. Certainly not everyone tends toward these extremes, but most of us haven't found the key to lasting change.

One young man comes to mind who had struggled for years with an easily triggered temper. His cutting remarks had devastated his wife more than once. When he could see the pain his anger produced, he felt profound remorse and desperately wanted to change. He tried everything. He gave himself to almost preoccupying involvement in Scripture and fervent prayer, often during early morning hours of sleeplessness. His work as an assistant pastor continued to be applauded. People loved him. But he felt like a hypocrite, a phony who looked good on the outside but was hopelessly corrupt on the inside.

The combination of prayer, Bible study, and church work had failed to resolve whatever beneath-the-waterline problems were erupting in outbursts of anger. In despair he said to me, "I don't know what else to do. I can't try harder to control my temper, and I'm already doing every Christian thing I know to do. But there's no power in my life. I don't know how to do better." Doing his Christian duties had not produced change on the inside.

Another man, this one a middle-aged businessman, was a competent Bible teacher, a tireless church worker, and a faithful prayer warrior. But no one, including his wife, could get close to him. His years of prayer and Bible study had made him into everything he should be—except a man of love. And the Apostle Paul makes it clear that without love our best efforts amount to very little. The man was committed to performing Christian duties, but he had no real power to draw anyone into a deeper, more passionate pursuit of God.

The conclusion is clear: More is involved in changing us on the inside than increased diligence on the outside. Using the model of the iceberg, this approach to changing from the inside out might be sketched this way:

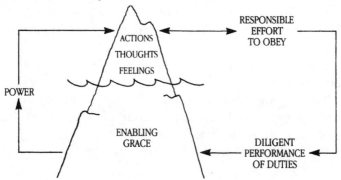

Option 2: Depend on the Special Work of the Holy Spirit

A second approach grants that more needs to be done to change than performing Christian duties and expecting the resulting grace to take care of below-the-waterline problems. The effects of the Fall and our stubborn inclination to sin must be more forcefully dealt with by a definite work of the Spirit. Certainly we must choose to do what's right and continue to learn more about God and His Word, but a special power is necessary and available to lift us to higher ground in our pursuit of godliness.

The mechanics of appropriating this power are understood differently by people who agree that the Holy Spirit must somehow be unleashed in a person's life. Some urge us to seek a second blessing or to be baptized in the Spirit as an experience subsequent to salvation. Evidences of a new dimension of spiritual reality such as speaking in tongues are thought to accompany the Spirit's special work.

Other teaching prepares us to unconditionally surrender our heart to God by convincing us of the impossibility of living as we should in our own strength. The decision to fully trust born of desperate necessity reflects a level of dependence on God that frees the Holy Spirit to work powerfully in our deepest being, enabling us to exhibit spiritual fruit.

Others emphasize John Wesley's report of being "strangely warmed." A richer capacity to love, they say, naturally develops when we enter more deeply into the truth of God's love for us.

Still others encourage us to reckon ourselves as co-crucified and co-resurrected with Christ to the point where we exchange our life for His. Holding to the truth of our identity in Christ and choosing to depend on the reality of His life present within us empowers us to live at a new level of victory.

The unifying theme of this second option for dealing with internal change is the belief that the Spirit of God can be released to do what needs to be done by some decisive act of faith on our part. Perhaps the idea can be sketched this way:

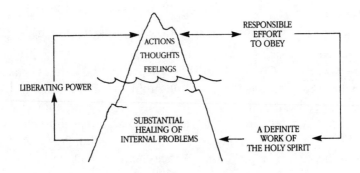

Option 3: Work Through Obstacles to Growth

Notice that neither of the first two options requires us to deal *directly* with issues below the waterline. Problems such as a fear of romantic involvement that began with sexual abuse in childhood or low self-esteem planted by inattentive parents or strong urges to do weird things do not need to be looked at, understood, and dealt with. The first approach assures us that commitment to do the right thing is all that's necessary. The power of God will come into our life as we perform our Christian duties. If we're struggling with depressed feelings, we need not take an inside look; we must simply become more involved in Bible study, prayer, and Christian service.

The second approach also assumes that it's not necessary to take an inside look. The Holy Spirit understands all that's inside and is able to clean up the mess if we permit Him to do His work. A long, hard, thorough look at our attitudes, feelings, goals, and self-image is at best self-absorbing introspection. All we must do in order to deeply change is to more fervently entrust ourselves to the Spirit.

Frustration with these approaches has opened the door to the modern emphasis on counseling, share groups, and seminars on self-understanding. Doing right or yielding to God's Spirit has not always produced the change we desired. Disappointed with traditional Christian approaches to change, we eagerly welcome new ideas. When blocks to growth are not overcome by more study or deeper yielding, some form of counseling sometimes seems appropriate.

I am a counselor. I have worked with hundreds of people and, I believe, have substantially helped many. I am sympathetic to our modern emphasis on counseling because most counselors (not all) encourage an honest look below the waterline. I regard that as a big plus. The tragedy is that counselors are often more aware of the importance of facing who we really are than are churches.

Until this situation changes, until communities of God's people are willing to courageously look at each other's lives and to search out God's answers for the tough questions, professional counseling will play a needed and vital role in promoting deep change. Unfortunately, individual counselors may not provide biblical solutions for their desperate clients. Unless the church begins to encourage an inside look as well, hurting people may find only false and temporary solutions.

Whether the help comes through healing memories, primal screaming, or Christianized psychotherapy, option 3 asserts that direct work on deeper issues beneath the waterline is essential to removing obstacles to growth. More often than not, however, psychological efforts do not resolve the deepest issues, which are spiritual. Change through counseling often involves *working through deep problems* rather than *repenting of deep sin*. The message is that power comes through self-awareness and psychological maturity. The God who works *in us,* giving us the will and power to change, is set aside as peripheral to real transformation. Let me sketch option 3 this way:

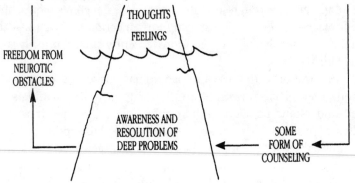

Dealing with our insides can be frustrating. Disciplined Christian living fails to resolve all the problems in our soul. Inviting the Holy Spirit to take over our life leaves part of our being untouched. Looking honestly at our insides with the help of a counselor leads sometimes to confusion and morbid self-preoccupation. But still our Lord requires us to clean the inside of our personalities before we can ever experience legitimate cleanliness on the outside. We must take an inside look if real change is to occur.

In the remainder of this book, I want to develop a framework for understanding "inside-out" change that can guide us through the joys and trials of life. An inside look can be frustrating, but we can do better than talk about two dogs barking for control of our life.

CHAPTER THREE

KNOWING WHAT TO LOOK FOR

Exploring the heart is both important and tricky business. When nervous feelings twist our stomach into knots, we want to know why. What is happening in our deceitful heart and foolish mind to create these awful feelings? An inside look is necessary but confusing. And within Christian circles there is little to help us in carefully searching through our insides to see what's wrong.[1]

For centuries, the church has assumed responsibility for the care and cure of souls, believing that only God can adequately deal with the corruption and loneliness of the human heart. But when Freud introduced the era of "depth psychology," churchmen began to wonder if their simple prescriptions of confession, forgiveness, and reconciliation were strong enough medicines to treat the newly identified complexities beneath the surface of people's lives. Such things as repressed emotions, fragmented egos, and psychosexual fixations seemed too much for the well-meaning but psychologically naive pastor.

In the mid 1900s, a movement took shape that has profoundly influenced our modern understanding of how to help people change. The church, uniquely equipped to respond to spiritual matters (such things as one's relationship to God and eternal destiny), turned to psychology for help in dealing with the mundane but often more urgent questions about getting along with oneself and others in this life. Behind this merger is the definite assumption that a depth understanding of ourselves is better achieved through the insights of psychology than through the wisdom of Scripture.

Efforts to figure out what's going on inside that depend on biblical ideas are regarded as a bit shallow, incisive perhaps in identifying spiritual problems like rebellion or unbelief, but weak in explaining the many personal problems we all face. To really understand your daughter's anorexia or your own lack of self-confidence, you must go outside the church, or at least to a pastor with psychological training.

The difficulty with this bias is that it's largely justified. Churches often have a woefully simplistic understanding of the problems people experience. A fair number seem to glory in their ignorance by insisting there is no need for an inside look. "Just morbid introspection," some say about any attempt at self-understanding. "If people would get into the Word, on their knees, and out into their neighborhoods witnessing for Christ, they would have no time for personal aches and pains. Forget all this psychological business of looking inside and get serious about your commitment to Christ."

The choice confronting many sincere, struggling Christians is either (1) to ignore the critical issues of internal character development and just try harder to be good Christians without ever understanding what's happening beneath the surface of their lives or (2) to take an inside look guided more by current psychological theory than by biblical revelation. Identifying your temperament, healing painful memories, learning to ventilate buried hurts, reconstructing the damaging impact of your parent's mistakes, facing destructive emotions and hidden agendas and bringing them under conscious control are all examples of the second alternative.

Neither of the two options moves us toward the kind of deep character change our Lord desires. If we are to change from the inside out, we must understand what internal problems need correction. That requires an inside look. And the inside look must be guided by the Bible's teaching on what to expect when we peel off the layers and explore what lurks beneath the surface. I submit that we're long overdue for an understanding of how to change that begins with an honest look at what we're like beneath the surface and is guided by the light of Scripture.

An inside look is important, but as already stated, it is tricky. The same Bible that instructs us to guard our heart (Proverbs 4:23) also tells us our heart is impossible to understand as well as deceitfully wicked (Jeremiah 17:9). The command to keep watch over our unknowable heart seems rather like ordering a guard to never let an invisible prisoner out of his sight.

Clearly, if our insides are as difficult to know as the Bible indicates, then any hope of an accurate inward look depends entirely on God's willingness to help. Students of the human personality can uncover mounds of data and organize their findings into intriguing and perhaps insightful theories, but without God's help, no effort to explore the heart will ever pinpoint the core problems that need changing.

The good news, of course, is that the opposite is also true. With God's help, we can understand what needs to be understood. When depression slowly erodes our energy, when strong urges to do wrong pop out of nowhere, when honest feedback makes it clear that we're not good at communicating love, we can and we must remain confident that the Bible will guide us in our inside look to whatever issues need our attention.

Deep Longings and Wrong Strategies

In the rest of this chapter, I want to get us started on our inward look.[2] A helpful place to begin is with a record of what God saw when He looked deeply into the hearts of His people during a time in their history when they were slipping far away from Him. Listen to His comments in Jeremiah 2:13:

> "My people have committed two sins: They have forsaken me, the spring of living water, and have dug their own cisterns, broken cisterns that cannot hold water."

Notice two observations the text suggests. First, *people are thirsty.* Although the fact of universal thirst is not directly stated, it is clearly assumed. Frequent references to thirsty hearts in the Bible, as well as to the fact that people were designed to enjoy satisfaction available only in God, support the idea that every person is thirsty. We all long for what God designed us to enjoy: tension-free relationships filled with deep, loving acceptance and with opportunities to make a difference to someone else. Observe carefully that in our text, God assumes His people are thirsty but He never condemns them for that thirst. Thirst is not the problem. Neither of the two sins He rebukes them for involves the fact that people are thirsty.

Second, *people are moving in wrong directions in response to their thirst.* They refuse to trust God to look after their thirst. Instead, they insist on maintaining control of finding their own satisfaction. They're all moving about determined to satisfy the longings of their hearts by picking up a shovel, looking for a likely spot to dig, and then searching for a fulfillment they can generate. To put it simply, people want to run their own lives. Fallen man is both terrified of vulnerability and committed to maintaining independence.

The human race got off on a seriously wrong foot when Eve yielded to Satan's lie that more satisfaction was available if she took matters into her own hands. When Adam joined her in looking for life outside of Gods revealed will, he infected all his descendants with the disease of self-management. Now no one seeks after God in an effort to find life. The most natural thing for us to do is to develop strategies for finding life that reflect our commitment to depending on our own resources. Simple trust is out of fashion. Self-protection has become the norm.

The Scriptures consistently expose people as both thirsty and foolish. We long for the satisfaction we were built to enjoy, but we all move away from God to find it. An inside look, then, can be expected to uncover two elements imbedded deeply in our heart: (1) thirst or *deep longings* for what we do not have; and (2) stubborn independence reflected in *wrong strategies* for finding the life we desire.

It is with an understanding of these two fundamental elements that we can productively explore beneath the surface of our everyday problems. The first element, *deep longings,* reflects our humanness and all the dignity accorded to us as bearers of God's image. We long for a quality of relationship and meaning that no other creature has the capacity to enjoy. We were designed to richly enjoy the person of God as well as His provisions.

The second element, *wrong strategies,* exists because we are sinful. Only foolish, rebellious, proud people would move away from the Source of life in search of a fulfillment they can control. And that is exactly what we've done—and do. Spouses demand certain responses from one another as a condition for life. People require that they never hurt again the way they once did in some previous trauma. We devise strategies designed to keep us warmly involved with each other at a safe distance. We live to gain life from others and to protect ourselves from whatever we think is life-threatening.

An inside look must anticipate uncovering deep, unsatisfied longings that bear testimony to our *dignity,* as well as foolish and ineffective strategies for keeping ourselves out of pain that reflect our *depravity.* Each of us is a glorious ruin. And the further we look into our heart, the more clearly we can see the wonder of our ability to enjoy relationship alongside the tragedy of our determination to arrange for our own protection from hurt.

Taking an Inside Look

One brief illustration may clarify how these two elements operate beneath the surface. A married couple wonders what to do with their twenty-two-year-old son who has dropped out of college with a drinking problem and wants to return home. The usual Christian approach to resolving their question would be to consult a few "experts" to see whether there's a consensus in how biblical principles might apply. After consulting with their advisors and praying that God would overrule any wrong decision they might make, they decide either to forbid their son to return home to teach him responsibility, or to welcome him back to demonstrate grace.

But suppose we were to take an inside look before arriving at the decision. Perhaps the young man's longings for respect and involvement have gone unmet in a family where Dad is distant, hostile, and uninvolved, and where Mom clings protectively to her son for the intimacy her husband denies her. In that situation, perhaps the son should be received home with both an apology from Dad for his cold distance and a commitment to learn how to warmly relate, and a commitment from Mom to healthily back away from her son as she learns to more openly share her pain with her husband.

In order to make these changes, both parents would need to look inside themselves to see their own unsatisfied thirst and their self-protective styles of relating. For example, Dad might need to face how deeply inadequate he feels to give of himself with any hope of finding respect. Perhaps *his* father never valued him for anything other than his work habits. As a result, he may have learned to work hard and give little of himself, hoping this style of relating would bring him everything he wanted. When his son began giving him trouble during his teen years, Dad likely withdrew into working harder, feeling anger at his son for letting him down but being unwilling to share openly his concern and affection for fear that what he shared of himself would not be well received by his son. His longings for respect and for relationship with his son are legitimate; his strategy of keeping his distance to protect himself from rejection is sinful.

Perhaps Mom, after years of living with a man who never gave himself to her, had become a hard woman, a mother who matter-of-factly performed her maternal duties. Her feminine soul may have been aching with the pain of loneliness and neglect, a pain so terrible that her only solution (in her mind) was to never again be close enough to anyone to be hurt. The deep love she felt for her son may have been hidden behind the barricade of self-protective coolness. To make it even more complex, perhaps Mom, although dutiful in her approach to mothering, yielded to her unquenchable desires for intimacy by becoming manipulatively involved with her son, much like Rebekah with Jacob. The boy may have felt unwanted by his father and controlled by his mother.

Without for a moment excusing his sinful behavior by focusing on his parent's failures, I would still want to see the family face their relational problems if the young man were to return home. If, on the other hand, the family was characterized by a soft-touch father who granted his sons every wish and a docile mother who could never say no to anything, then it might be wise to require certain evidence of responsibility in their son before offering to welcome him home.

No amount of looking inside will yield perfect certainty about what to do. But some understanding of what is going on within us will often help us see what changes must occur on the inside before effective external change can be expected.

In Part Two, I want to explore the deep longings of the human heart and, in Part Three, how we come up with wrong strategies to deal with them. Part Four suggests the biblical means for shifting direction from protecting ourselves to pursuing God. And that shift, as we will see later, is the core of change from the inside out.

NOTES

1. For a more complete discussion of my understanding of the human personality, see *Understanding People* (Grand Rapids: Zondervan, 1987).

2. I have written a more technical explanation of what is inside, with documented biblical support, in *Understanding People* (Grand Rapids: Zondervan, 1987).

PART TWO
WE'RE THIRSTY PEOPLE

"I don't want to admit it, but I know something's wrong."

CHAPTER FOUR

"IF ANYONE IS THIRSTY. . ."

If we are to become people who *know* God, who taste Him with a richness that sustains us through hard times of rejection and loss, then we must take an inside look. In the minds of thousands of Christians, the route to abundant living and spiritual maturity requires only that we become disciplined students of God's Word, people who faithfully and fervently pray, eager witnesses of the gospel who seize opportunities to tell others about Christ, and tireless church members willing to give our time, talents, and tithes to the local church.

Many wish they were doing better in their Christian responsibilities. They live with a mixture of guilt for not measuring up and assume their problems could be resolved if they exerted more effort to live as they should.

Others have tried their hardest and failed. After giving their best efforts to doing all they think they should do, they sit numbly in church going through the motions of worship, while feeling cheated, pressured, disillusioned, and wondering what other hoops God requires them to jump through before He'll straighten out their lives and make them happy.

Still others—and I suspect they're the majority—regard zealous commitment to Bible study, prayer, witnessing, and service as appropriate for the specially called. Jeremiah was chosen before he was born. Paul was called through a blinding encounter with a heavenly light. Pastors are set apart for unique service by ordination. But ordinary folks need only be friendly to people, faithful to their spouses, hard-working in their jobs, and balanced in their distribution of time between family, church, and personal leisure. Churches are filled with folks who, as long as they think about their lives only during commercial breaks on television and polite Bible studies, are really quite content, pleased with themselves, and perhaps a bit smug in their gratitude to God for His blessings.

Two categories of Christians emerge: those who have high standards of commitment and those who are content to live ordinary, respectable lives. The first group includes people who are frustrated with their inability to measure up to their lofty ideals and a few who are satisfied with their performance. The second group consists mostly of folks who live reasonably happy lives as long as money, health, and relationships are doing well. If things fall apart, they scramble to restore a measure of order to their lives. If that proves impossible, then a search for alternative sources of comfort begins. When available comfort is exceeded by inescapable suffering, then bitterness, depression, and a commitment to escape develop.

Our Lord severely rebuked people whose lives merely conformed to scrupulously high standards of religious conduct (Matthew 23:13-36). With scathing insight that seems obvious when we think about the Pharisees but is uncomfortably penetrating when the focus shifts to us, Christ exposed the dirt hidden beneath an outwardly religious, moral, disciplined life. Notice carefully that a zeal for measuring up to standards did not produce the kind of life our Lord commended. And the ordinary people, folks who were more relaxed than committed, made the Lord gag. "I know your deeds, that you are neither cold nor hot. I wish you were either one or the other! So, because you are lukewarm—neither hot nor cold—I am about to spit you out of my mouth" (Revelation 3:15-16).

Outside cleanliness, whether the product of zeal or of complacency, does not impress our Lord. With relentless penetration,

He intends to deal with the filth we try to keep hidden beneath the surface. To live life as God intends requires that we uncover the dirt and learn what we must do to participate in the cleaning process. We must take an inside look.

Two Reactions

For people who are disillusioned and discouraged after years of trying hard to do everything right, the news is good: more effort isn't the answer. But folks who are satisfied either with their zealous conformity to Christian standards or with their nicely balanced and comfortably moral approach to life need to be directly confronted with the Lord Jesus Christ's insistence that internal matters be addressed. For them, the news is threatening.

When a psychologist urges people to introspect, Christians in our culture typically react in one of two ways. Some immediately hear a call to self-preoccupation and worry that the local churches will begin dividing into self-discovery groups that become so engrossed by personal aches and pains that their concern for reaching out to others is quickly lost.

Others respond with appreciation. Perhaps, they hope, a focus on deep needs will free people from the stifling legalism of a "do this, do that" Christianity and will help them extend a message of affirmation to the countless people who struggle to accept themselves.

Before we actually begin our inside look, I want to clearly state that I'm comfortable with neither reaction. The first one, which fears that self-understanding leads to self-centeredness, often builds on the assumption that personal problems dissolve in the solution of Bible knowledge and Christian activities. Sin is treated as nothing more than deliberate behavioral violation of God's standards. We're told that a quick and superficial look at our life is all that's needed to see where we're going wrong. Extended exploration of our heart is simply not needed and can be positively harmful. Stronger commitment to do right is the key to victorious living.

The second reaction, which centers completely on the importance of self-acceptance as the foundation for abundant living, does

Conformity to Christian standards and happiness in life are byproducts ...of maturity

not define sin *superficially* as mere behavioral transgression, but it defines sin *wrongly* as an inability to trust God enough to love oneself. People's problems are thought to be rooted more in a lack of affirmation than in deep and stubborn sinfulness. From this perspective, the product of an inside look is not genuine repentance, but a clear realization of one's value.

The Purpose of an Inside Look

It is my view that an inside look is necessary as we continue to live responsibly before God, but that its direct purpose is not to promote self-acceptance. As this chapter will begin to make clear, an inside look can help me to face my dependency on God in a manner that requires me to grapple with what it means to deeply trust. It can also expose my determination, in all its subtle ugliness, to manage life on my own. Such exposure pushes me toward deeper repentance and more thorough obedience.

The goal of change from the inside out is neither conformity to Christian standards nor increasing levels of happiness. Both conformity and happiness must develop as byproducts of maturity. Real change produces maturity, that rare type of character that makes it possible to genuinely love. People who offer a quality of relationship that strikes deep into the souls of others are mature. And developing maturity requires an inside look.

A greater capacity to draw others to Jesus Christ through the depth of our love, which real change develops, does not come about through disciplined efforts to do the right things or through small group interaction designed to help us accept ourselves more completely. Neither approach gets at the dirt beneath the surface. Neither approach exposes how our limited efforts to love are deeply stained with subtle self-protection. Neither approach will help us change from the inside out. We need to honestly look deep inside and deal with the real flaws in our makeup.

In the last chapter, I suggested that two major biblical themes could serve as adequate guides for our inside look: people are *thirsty* and people are *foolish*. As image-bearers designed to enjoy God and everything He has made, we are thirsty people who long for what was lost in the Fall. As fallen people who have declared our intention to find life apart from God, we devise foolish, ineffective, and immoral strategies to provide for our own satisfaction. As we pull back the layers of our lives to see what's underneath, we can expect to find both longings—some of which are profoundly deep—and strategies for satisfying those longings that reflect our effort to handle life on our own. Look with me first at our longings.

Dealing with Our Desires

No more than a moment's reflection is required to put us in touch with the fact that we want certain things. We want to feel a certain way; we want people to make us feel good by the way they treat us; we want job and financial opportunities that bring us pleasure and security; we want to know we matter to someone and belong somewhere; we want pleasant weather for our Saturday afternoon picnic. If we could stop time at any given point in our day, it wouldn't be difficult to pinpoint some desire providing motivation for what we're doing.

Often, when Christian people admit to themselves that they're wanting something, they immediately feel selfish. "I'm just thinking of myself. I know I shouldn't be concerned with whether things go my way. I should care more about the needs of others." And so they pray God will help them get over their selfishness.

But even after fervent prayer and concerted efforts to behave more selflessly, it's difficult to deny the fact that deep personal desires remain. Prayer to "get over" our longings is not effective. The only way to overcome these desires is to treat them as though they don't exist and to forcefully choose to put others ahead of ourselves.

When we try to forget about ourselves in the quest for an other-centered maturity, the tendency is to develop a machine-like approach to relationships ("I will do what is best for you regardless of how I feel"), which warms our friends about as much as good wishes from a flight attendant warm passengers as they exit the airplane. Those who are honest enough to admit the continued, almost urgent, presence of desires sometimes work even harder to drive them away through spiritual means: more time in the Word, longer prayer lists, more church committees.

But still desires remain. And that's good. We can't deny our inside desires without losing touch with a very real part of our existence. Wives do want their husbands to treat them well. Husbands do want their wives to respect them. Parents do want their kids to come home by curfew. Singles do want to form meaningful relationships that go beyond fun times.

What are we to do with these stubborn desires that simply will not go away? Should we regard them as emerging from our sinful nature and therefore work to live apart from their influence? Or should we go to the other extreme, call them legitimate, and embrace a theology that encourages confidence that God will satisfy every desire of our heart?

A woman's husband left her for a younger mistress after thirty years of marriage. She wanted him back. What should she do? The first line of thinking would have instructed her to set aside her desire for reconciliation and directed her toward the opportunities for friendship and service that God provides. The second idea would urge her to name what she really wants and trust God to bring it about. The choice seems to be between a stoic denial of desires and a manipulative approach to Christianity that guarantees satisfaction of desires. We can either become a machine ourselves or make God into a vending machine that gives us what we want.

There must be a better alternative. Somehow the reality of internal desires must be handled in such a way that we compromise neither our personal vitality nor the Lord's command to love one another. Change from the inside out moves us toward both (1) a passionate awareness of longings that keeps us warm-blooded and real, and (2) a non-demanding style of relating that frees us to genuinely care about others.

The key, I suggest, to dealing honestly with our desires without losing personal authenticity or genuine concern about others is to understand two facts about our desires. First, our desires, though energizing a complex variety of sinful directions, are related not only to our fallenness but also, and more profoundly, to our humanness. In other words, *it's okay to desire.* Second, when we look carefully at what we deeply desire, we come to realize that what we want is simply not available, not until heaven. The more aware we become of our most passionate longings, the more lonely and sad we feel. A colleague has described the experience as feeling "out of the nest."

Both errors in responding to our longings—hiding them in a flurry of Christian activity and focusing on them to find satisfaction—deny the simple truth that we legitimately want what we cannot have in this world. We were designed to live in a perfect world uncorrupted by the weeds of disharmony and distance. Until we take up residence in that world, however, we will hurt. It is, therefore, not only okay to desire, *but also okay to hurt.*

Beneath the obvious struggles of everyday life, thirsty souls pant after satisfaction. We must recognize how the reality of unquenched thirst surfaces in our life. Think with me first about our legitimate desires that we rarely recognize.

It's Okay to Desire

Some time ago, my wife and I were on our way to our favorite pizza restaurant. In the back seat of the car was another couple, good friends. I was at the wheel, feeling quite confident in my ability not only to drive the car competently but also to find the restaurant. I'd been there many times before.

I approached Second Avenue, driving east on Glades Road. The restaurant was located a mile north on Second Avenue, requiring that I turn left from Glades. I therefore eased the car into the left-hand lane, stopped because the light was red, and pressed the left-hand turn signal.

After a few moments of waiting, the light turned green. Before I had a chance to put my plan into action, my wife said, "Take a left here, honey."

Five simple words—*take a left here, honey*—and I felt furious. I jerked my head toward her, snapped, "I know," and stepped on the gas. Everything in me wanted to turn right but my desire for pizza out-weighed my desire for revenge, so I turned left. Words flooded my mind, begging for release through my mouth, expressions of something other than appreciation for her help. Because the other people in the car were seeing me for counseling, I chose not to share those words with my wife.

I felt angry, far more so than my wife's apparent lack of confidence in my navigational skills seemed to justify. I could have honestly stated that I was deeply committed to my wife, but at that moment the commitment was barren of emotional warmth.

Under my capable direction, we drove down Second Avenue until we saw the huge, well-lit sign that announced "Pizza." Just as I prepared to turn, my wife pointed and said, "Here it is!" My rage doubled. Why? Certainly a host of questions, some a bit threatening, emerges from this rather ordinary incident:

> ➤ What does the intensity of my anger say about my level of maturity?
> ➤ Was my wife really not sure I knew where I was going, or was she acting out of casual habit and a real desire to be helpful?
> ➤ How should a husband best handle angry emotions toward his wife? Discuss it later? Label himself too sensitive and forget it? Get things in perspective by rehearsing her good points? Spew out his feelings in the name of honesty? Repent of his anger and ask God's help to be warm?

Most attempts to think through a common marital tension like this one fail to probe deeply enough into the real roots of the problem. Exhortations to overlook it and be less touchy or to communicate openly about feelings in an effort to promote mutual understanding ignore a penetrating question that needs to be asked: *What do I deeply desire that was not provided in that interaction?* "Here we go—typical psychologist. More introspection and less responsibility. Just do what you should and get on with living."

Perhaps an inward look could uncover a more fundamental flaw that, if corrected, could lead to better husbanding. A look directed at my desires makes it plain that I want to be *respected*. To say I *long for respect* does not put the matter too strongly. I long to know that someone sees something in me that's valuable, that my existence is important because I'm capable of making a difference. Many people refer to this longing as a desire for significance or, more specifically, personal meaningfulness. I like it when people take me seriously, when they follow up a comment I make with questions to probe what I meant and what I feel. It touches something deep within me when people still want to hear from me even after I make a stupid remark. I want to be treated with respect not just when I do well, but also when I stumble.

The longing is legitimate and must not be ignored by focusing on my responsibility to treat my wife kindly. To deny the longing is to neglect a part of me that God made. When God instructed Adam to tend the garden, He provided Adam with meaningful activity. Adam was not assigned a "We'll-make-you-feel-important" kind of job. Adam's work was important. He made a difference. With non-programmed freedom, Adam's choice to obey was the condition for keeping things as they should be. When he exercised his freedom to rebel, he made an impact that has shaken the world from that day to this.

The fact that I long to matter reflects both (1) my Creator's wisdom and kindness in designing me with freedom, and (2) the separation between God and me introduced by sin. If we had never sinned, we would live with a wonderful realization of our part in God's world rather than a desperate desire to find meaning. My desire for respect is tied both to my fallenness and to my humanity. Although my deep longings do not exist unstained by sin, it is still accurate to state that I want to be respected because I was built to matter. When I perceive that I'm disrespected, I react in my soul just as my toe reacts when a heavy-footed person steps on it. I hurt.

When my wife seems not to respect my ability to accomplish a simple task, that deep part of me that longs to be regarded as adequate feels pain. I can no more eliminate the pain than I can pretend my stepped-on toe does not hurt. My toe was built for better treatment than it sometimes receives. And I was built for respect. I cannot change that fact. But more than respect, I was designed for *relationship.* I want someone to be involved with me who is strong enough to handle everything about me without retreating or feeling threatened.

Most of us are terrified to be open with each other, not because we're afraid of hurting or discouraging people, but because we profoundly fear that others will retreat from us. We hate to admit that the people we depend on are simply too weak to stay deeply involved once they face all that we are. We don't want to accept the fact that, since the Fall, no human being has the capacity to love us perfectly.

One young woman told me that whenever she hinted to her father that she struggled both with her faith and with sexual temptation, he would artfully—and quickly—change the subject. The message was clear: "I do not feel comfortable in knowing certain things about you, so do not tell me." The effect on his daughter was to create a terrible fear that no one could ever handle all that was inside her. She learned to be deeply afraid of any thoughts or feelings that might threaten others if she expressed them. In her efforts to run from whatever could be unnerving to others, her normal doubts and urges were strengthened, causing her to feel overwhelmed by questions about God and desires for sexual pleasure. Doubt and lust became overpowering obsessions she could not escape. Beneath it all was a terribly frustrated longing to have someone see all of her and remain deeply involved.

It does no good to remind ourselves that our family and friends mean well. Try as we may, we cannot rid ourselves of the desire to have what no one has given. We are dependent by nature. We require resources outside ourselves if we're to enjoy either physical or personal life. We literally and absolutely need someone stronger than we are to look after us and to provide for us what we were designed to enjoy. God intended that we warmly respond to the loving strength of another, and what we were built to enjoy, we deeply desire. His plan really is quite simple. Adam and Eve were to turn to God as the strong one on whom they could depend and *then* to each other to both enjoy what the other uniquely provided and to give of themselves to enhance the other's pleasure.

We long for both respect and involvement, impact and relationship. We are thirsty for what our soul thrives on. In the desert
of a fallen world, our soul is parched. We receive neither respect
nor involvement to the degree we deeply crave.

Our Lord Jesus walked into a group of people whose ritualistic
practice of religion had so numbed their souls that they no longer
were conscious of unsatisfied desires. To move them from lifeless
ceremony toward the vitality of knowing God, He stood up and
shouted, "If anyone is thirsty, let him come to me and drink" (John
7:37). There was no thought that perhaps some were thirsty and
others were not. Every fallen person created to enjoy God is thirsty.
But many—perhaps most—of the people Jesus invited were
unaware of their thirst. Perhaps they had given up hope of ever
finding satisfaction and had successfully turned their attention away
from that ache inside. By focusing on other matters, thirsty people
can sometimes become oblivious to their parched souls.

When our Lord encouraged the Jews to admit their thirst, it
must have terrified a few. How cruel to promise water to a dying
man and then hold up empty hands. Our Lord knew His hands
were not empty, that He could supply the water the people wanted,
but could they trust Him? Perhaps, in their minds, He was offering something He couldn't provide. Everyone has had experiences
with people who promise more than they deliver. Was this to be
one more relationship that would prove disappointing? How risky
to believe someone when they offer what we desperately want but
fear no one has.

"Your hearts long for so much you do not have. You want to
know your lives have meaning, whether you fail or succeed as a
parent. You want someone to ask probing questions about you,
unafraid to see who you really are, strong enough to remain lovingly involved no matter what they find. If anyone is thirsty ... "

I can imagine a few brave souls running to Jesus, overwhelmed
by the reality of their thirst. "Yes, Lord, I am thirsty. I admit it. No
one has touched me as I long to be touched. I deeply desire what
I do not have."

"If anyone is thirsty...." What did He say next? Notice He
did not say: "Good! I'm glad you admit it. Now stop being so

selfish. Repent of your thirst and get on with loving others. Bury your hurt under renewed commitment to stay productively busy, and by the way, keep a safe distance from people. If you get too close you'll be hurt again and that could make you focus too much on yourself."

Nor did He say: "Now that you're in touch with your thirst, I want you to explore it deeply. Get together with the other folks in your church who admit their desires and study what can be done to feel better."

What He said was: "Come!" Neither deny your thirst nor focus on it. Christ's invitation to come to Him on the basis of perceived thirst grants legitimacy to the longings of our soul. *It's okay to desire.*

It's Okay to Hurt

A second point needs to be made, one that's closely related to the first. We long for what we cannot have until God arranges things to His standards. Nothing less than perfect relationships in a perfect world among perfect people will make pain-free happiness a reality.

A good friend of mine, a well-respected theologian, listened to me lecture to a seminary class four hours per week for two entire semesters. He patiently endured extended discussions on the philosophy of knowledge, sat without complaint through a lengthy attempt to define what it means to bear God's image, and graciously considered my thoughts on how sin has ruined things and what can be done to undo the damage.

On a pleasant day in late spring, I presented my final lecture. The students filed out, rubbing their wrists to restore circulation lost through furious note-taking and making plans to review the class material before the exam. I felt happily spent, confident that the complexity of all I said had not obscured a few important themes I wanted my students to grasp.

As I walked down the hallway with my theologian friend, he looked thoughtful as he said, "I've appreciated your two courses a great deal and have reflected seriously on what you've said. I think most people, including myself, are leaving with the rather novel idea that it's really okay for Christians to hurt."

My immediate reaction was to feel a bit offended. I had just poured out my mind and soul in a comprehensive attempt to lay out a framework for counseling—and he'd reduced it all to one simple thought.

A few days later he added, "I think you also got across a second idea, that sin is a far bigger problem than most of us think." That was small encouragement. Nearly ninety hours of lectures were now compressed (or expanded?) into two thoughts rather than one: *It's okay to hurt, and sin is a bigger problem than we think.*

While nursing a mildly wounded ego, it occurred to me that those two thoughts may actually be central to understanding and helping people. The second one will be discussed in chapters 7, 8, and 9. The first idea, that it's okay to hurt, is an obvious but important truth for imperfect people who were built for perfection to grasp. Let me discuss why this truth is so vital to understand.

A young man was told at age twenty-seven that his father's untimely death twenty-two years earlier had been the result of suicide. The five-year-old son had been told that his father suffered an unexpected heart attack. He'd believed that story ever since.[1] An older cousin, who knew what had happened but didn't know my client had been deliberately misinformed, casually referred one day to the father's suicide so many years ago. The truth then came out that his mother had been exposed in an affair with another man and had subsequently announced her intention of divorcing the boy's father. Rather than face the pain of a broken marriage, one night soon after the news had surfaced, the father stumbled to the bathroom in the early morning and swallowed every pill he could find. He was found dead the next morning in the guest-room bed.

When my client learned the truth, a violent torrent of confusion, horror, and bitterness raged through his soul. For years now his mother had been remarried to the "other man," someone he had comfortably called Dad for more than twenty years. How could he go home to visit? What could be done with the overwhelming emotions he felt?

When he was thirty, three years after hearing the truth of his father's suicide, he consulted me. He reported that since that time, his one goal was to overcome or at least reduce the pain in his heart. Because he was a committed Christian, things like drinking, although tempting, were out. He felt reluctant to allow himself to become close to anyone, especially a woman, and therefore shared his burden with no one.

The only method he'd found that could soothe his throbbing soul was Bible memorization. The concentration required to commit long passages to memory, coupled occasionally with the content of what he would memorize, seemed to distract him sufficiently to provide relief. In his understanding of things, he was turning to God for help. He was renewing his mind through time in the Word. Whenever the image of his distraught father recklessly grabbing bottles of pills crowded into his mind, whenever thoughts of his mother's sinfulness and deceit flooded him with bitterness toward her and her current husband, he quickly reached for his Bible and memorized more verses. For three years now, he'd been following this procedure. As a result, he was nervous. His life presented him with a level of pain he was determined not to feel.

If it's true that each of us desperately desires what none of us has, then we're all in exactly the same dilemma as this unfortunate young man. The details of our life may be different, often less bizarre, but there is an emptiness in the core of our being we simply do not want to face. Its source could be a father who never took the time to ask us questions, a mother who made us feel helpless through her overprotection, a spouse for whom we can never be enough, friends who care only up to a point, or children who break our heart by their indifference to God. The stories are varied, but the theme is the same: We have all felt profoundly disappointed in every key relationship we've ever had. Therefore, we hurt.

It's clear that the purpose of the young man's obsession with Bible memorization was *not* to know God at any cost. His purpose was to relieve pain. Nothing is wrong, of course, with shaking the stone out of our shoe before continuing a walk. When relieving pain is not our final purpose in life, then it's reasonable to make ourselves as comfortable as a responsible and moral approach to life permits. *But when relief of the inevitable pain of living in a fallen world becomes our priority, at that moment we leave the path toward pursuing God.* God's prescriptions for handling life do not relieve an ache that is not meant to cease this side of heaven; they enable us to be faithful in the midst of it. Sometimes, the path of obedience even intensifies the pain in ways that seem entirely unfair, and even unkind of God.

Facing the Pain of Life

Behind our irresponsible and sinful response to life is a commitment to eliminate the pain of this world. That commitment is nourished by the fear that facing the pain would utterly destroy all hope for happiness. If we are to preserve our life at all, we must relieve the ache in our soul that comes from unsatisfied longings. That's how we think. We're wrong, but when the pain of rejection, isolation, failure, and weakness begins to creep into our stomach, it feels like the approach of death. Our very survival seems to depend on numbing the pain and finding some way to feel better. Eating, memorizing the Bible, masturbating, cleaning the bathroom, joining the church choir—we've got to do something to avoid the paralyzing ache we fear so deeply.

Although I'm not for a moment suggesting we should morbidly tune in to every ache we can identify in our soul, I am suggesting that to work at avoiding the experience of a certain amount of inevitable pain represents a denial of reality. None of us is fully enjoying what we thirst for. People let us down. We let people down. The simple fact we must face is this: *something is wrong with everything.* No matter how closely we walk with the Lord, we cannot escape the impact of a disappointing and sometimes evil world. A core sadness that will not go away is evidence not of spiritual immaturity, but of honest living in a sad world.

So many Christians sense a pressure to feel good. Although I appreciate the need for discretion in sharing deeply personal matters, I wish more Christian leaders would more openly discuss their struggles. I have no desire to hear details about a pastor's immorality, but I would like to hear leaders who are living outwardly decent and commendable lives tell of their battles with insensitivity and pride (sins every bit as serious as immorality) and their struggles with fear and fatigue. I'm encouraged when other Christians tell me of their doubts, frustrations, and discouragements. I discover I'm not alone, and I draw hope from others who are learning how God can meet them in their struggles.

Certainly it's easy to exaggerate the matter of transparency to the point where we dwell more on our problems than on the beauty of Christ. But too often the "public" Christians present their lives in a way that leaves the rest of us wondering what's wrong, why *we* hurt and worry and get mad when the preacher never does. The message that comes across to millions of Christians is that relief from pain and something approaching sinless perfection is available. It is possible, they teach, to experience a level of joy that swallows up all hurt. Paradise now, and more of it later.

We must remember that our Lord's promise of paradise today was given to a man about to die. When He addressed those who had more time left on earth, He spoke not of bliss but of failure, persecution, and hardship:

> ➤ "You will disown me three times!" (John 13:38)
> ➤ "I will show him how much he must suffer for my name." (Acts 9:16)
> ➤ "Everyone who wants to live a godly life in Christ Jesus will be persecuted." (2 Timothy 3:12)

The promise of health and wealth is real—but it is not for now. The situation is something like a doctor comforting a woman in labor with the words, "You will soon be holding your baby in your arms." First the pain—unrelievable and hard—then the pleasure. Tears for the night, joy in the morning. "Don't let your hearts be troubled," Jesus told His grieving disciples. "In a little while— not now—you will see the home I'm preparing for you. For the rest of your lives, you will have the strength of My presence and the joy of My promise, but life will be hard. You will hurt. But then .... happiness beyond description. Trust Me."

We long for what we were designed to enjoy: *It's okay to desire.* And we want what we cannot have until heaven: *It's okay to hurt.* "If anyone is thirsty, let him come to me."

I am thirsty. I long for what I do not have. What does it mean to come to Christ? I'm already a Christian. Insofar as I know my heart, I do want to follow Him. What am I to do with all these unsatisfied desires in my soul? How do I trust Him with my ache in a way that frees me to more deeply love?

To answer these questions, we must look closely at our Lord's promise to make streams of living water flow from within us.

NOTES

1. Every illustration I use throughout this book is drawn from my personal contact with clients and friends, but everyone is disguised. When I refer to a young man age twenty-seven I might be thinking of a teenage girl or a middle-aged housewife. In other words, I am not referring to the person who comes to mind as you read the story.

CHAPTER FIVE

SPRINGS OF LIVING WATER?
THEN WHY SO MUCH PAIN?

A man opened a counseling session with an urgent request: "I want to feel better quick."

I paused for a moment, then replied, "I suggest you get a case of your favorite alcoholic beverage, find some cooperative women, and go to the Bahamas for a month."

Now it was his turn to pause. He stared at me, looking puzzled, then asked, "Are you a Christian?"

"Why do you ask?"

"Well, your advice doesn't sound very biblical."

"It's the best I can do given your request. If you really want to feel good right away and get rid of any unpleasant emotion, then I don't recommend following Christ. Drunkenness, immoral pleasures, and vacations will work far better. Not for long, of course, but in the short run they'll give you what you want."

Preachers all across America are building huge congregations on the promise of unblemished happiness now. Our modern understanding of Christian joy envisions an eager excitement as we face each day, yielding to a serene warmth in older years, capped off with the bliss of heaven forever.

The biblical writers see things differently. Faith is required because life can be overwhelmingly confusing. Hope for a better day is all we can cling to in those honest moments of facing life's disappointments. And love is the only approach to life that achieves God's purposes and gives us a sense of relationship with Christ and others. Faith, hope, and love in the midst of a difficult world—that's a different understanding of what to expect from life than the view that promises we can always feel good.

But our Lord did speak of springs of living water bubbling up in the souls of people who come to Him. What did He mean? Apparently there's more to Christian living than well-handled pain.

Defining the Abundant Life

My life is characterized rather often by pleasant experiences. I enjoy flopping on a couch for a couple of hours with a good book, spending an evening with friends, playing golf on a crisp autumn day, joining people I love at the dinner table.

What I do for a living brings me immense satisfaction. There are, of course, plenty of frustrations. People and their problems sometimes feel like a flooded river in which I'm struggling unsuccessfully to keep afloat. Occasionally I feel like I'm going under for the third time. But the waters eventually subside, I reach land, and I return to teaching classes, writing books, traveling to seminars, and talking to people about their lives. And most of the time I really love what I do.

My family and friends are also sources of real joy. Everyone's relationships have their share of tensions—sometimes severe and prolonged—and mine are no exception. But many relationships in my life are working well enough to elicit deep gratitude and warm feelings.

In any group of Christians, a fair number would report a similar experience of life: creature comforts, meaningful work, good relationships. We all know the person who has lived for wealth and success, who's got it all, and who still admits to a terrible emptiness. But many of us have elements of the good life *plus* a Christian package of sincere commitment, moral integrity, and church involvement that helps us avoid the feeling that something is missing.

Is that style of life what Christ promised when He spoke of rivers of living water flowing through us? If we were honest, I suspect most of us would like to believe that personal comfort and spiritual commitment define the abundant life Jesus provides. I like comfort. I'm genuinely glad when my sons are doing well and my wife and I are thoroughly enjoying one another. I look forward to a good meal with friends. But I know that something deeper in me requires more—so I work on my relationship with God by renewing my commitment and reflecting on His Word. And when I'm enjoying both personal comfort and spiritual commitment, I really do feel pretty good. But the question must be asked: is that what springs of living water provide?

Many churches, particularly the ones that televise their services, make a habit of inviting only those whose lives are going well at the moment to share what Christ means to them. The message is consistent: comfort and commitment, both are available. Trust God to change whatever makes you uncomfortable while you choose to follow Him.

I have often wondered how much crippling guilt and soul-wracking pain those testimonies provoke in those who have committed themselves to Christ as best they can but whose lives are filled with terrible discomfort. As the speakers tell their stories of warm family reunions, children preparing for missionary service, relational tensions that have been replaced by joyful reconciliation, and financial losses that God has miraculously turned around, how many hearts rejoice in God's goodness?

What does the woman feel whose husband of thirty years left her three years ago and is now openly living with a girl half his age? Hope? Confusion? Bitterness? What do the grandparents feel who can't spend time with their grandchildren because the girl their son married has taken an unexplained disliking to them? Or what about the single person who's sick of the fun-and-games mentality of her church's singles group and yearns for meaningful adult relationships? Is she blessed by the testimonies of people who praise God for their personal comforts and humbly thank Him for winning them to strong commitment? Or does she quietly give up hope of finding real joy?

Most of us, even people like me who do enjoy many legitimate pleasures and who are sincerely committed to pursuing Christ, must admit to a host of unanswered questions, real disappointments, and a nagging emptiness that even our best relationship never relieves. Are we to ignore these internal realities and focus instead on the blessings of personal comfort as we work to honor our Christian commitment? I fear that most people whose lives provide enough pleasures to escape having to think about those troubling questions and emotions do precisely that. And those folks whose struggles are more pressing—broken marriages, rebellious kids, aching loneliness—well, we can only pray that God will restore their personal comforts as they continue to trust Him.

This kind of response turns church into a country club offering its benefits to those who are fortunate enough and well-mannered enough to qualify for membership. We sit Sunday after Sunday enjoying the fellowship of others who are comfortable and committed while the brokenhearted and poor press their noses against the window, looking in at us with resentment, envy, and despair.

If we are to become a community of deeply changed people, we must not only admit to our thirst, we must also carefully explore what Christ promised to do about that thirst. Did He promise to bring us comfort through enjoyable relationships, rewarding careers, and pleasurable activities—provided, of course, that we honor some level of commitment to Him? Or is the abundant life of bubbling springs a very different matter? Is it possible to have absolutely no rich communication with your husband, yet still taste those cool waters? Can a parent whose young adult son is far from the Lord know something real about peace and rest?

Our Lord has promised to flood our innermost being with springs of living water. If His words do not guarantee our personal comfort in exchange for spiritual commitment—and I don't think they do—then what is He saying? If He's promised springs of living water to all who come, then why do many sincere Christians live lives filled with pain?

I am convinced that change from the inside out can put us in vital touch with the reality of His promise. To adequately understand how we can be freed to drink deeply from His well, we must more thoroughly discuss the longings of our soul.

Three Kinds of Longings

Crucial
Critical
Casual

When our Lord promised to supply us with living water, He told us the springs would flow from our innermost being. The word translated "innermost being" or, in some versions, "belly," refers to a hollow place located centrally within us. Another meaning of the same word is appetite. In other words, Christ was promising to do something about the core desires of our soul. There are, of course, other desires that are important in varying degrees, but His words offer no guarantee for their satisfaction this side of heaven.

Think of the basic and most profound longings of the human heart, those desires that must be met if life is to be worth living, and call them *crucial longings.* We were designed to live in relationship with Someone unfailingly strong and lovingly involved who enables us to fulfill the important jobs He assigns. Without relationship or impact, life is profoundly empty. Nothing can fill that hollow core except what we were built to experience. Not imperfect friends, not impressive work, not excitement, not pleasure. Nothing can satisfy our crucial longings except the kind of relationship that only God offers.

But if we have crucial longings, it follows that we must also experience non-crucial longings. Divide these into two categories and call them *critical longings* and *casual longings.*

Everyone is aware of desires other than the deep longings that only God can meet, and some of those desires seem critically important. For example, the desire to be loved and respected by your mate, the hope that your children will remain close to you and live happy, responsible lives, the longing for friends who know how to be there when you need them. I think of *critical longings* as the legitimate and important desires for quality relationships that add immeasurably to the enjoyment of living.

A third category of desires, *casual longings,* includes every other desire we experience, ranging from the trivial ("I hope this restaurant has my favorite salad dressing") to the significant ("I want to hear a good report from my doctor"). The word *casual* might misrepresent what I want to communicate. Some desires I'm calling casual may feel acutely meaningful; for example, a clean bill of health when danger signs have caused alarm. The feature that discriminates between casual and critical longings, in my view, is the issue of personal relationship. If the longing does not centrally involve what can be supplied only through another person's giving of himself, then I choose to call the longing casual. If the desire can be met only through relationship with someone, I think of it as critical. And if that relational longing is so deep and central that only the resources of God will do, then that longing for relationship can rightly be called crucial.

The Consequences of Unsatisfied Longings

The importance of sorting our longings into these three categories begins to be evident when we consider the consequences of their frustration. When casual longings are not satisfied, we experience *manageable discomfort.* Although the discomfort may sometimes be excruciating, nothing central to my existence *as a person* is threatened if casual longings remain unmet. (The possibility of death threatens physical, not personal, existence.) When that happens I can pull myself together and continue on, sometimes easily, sometimes only with great difficulty. Christians and nonChristians can find the resources within their humanity to live reasonably effective lives when casual longings go unmet.

Critical longings are another story. When what I do seems unimportant, when evidence mounts that I'm not able to do what matters deeply to me, when people I care about don't care about me, when I suffer the loss of a relationship that deeply mattered, I feel a horrible emptiness within that hurts. Physical pain can sometimes be easier to bear than the anguish of loneliness, rejection, or failure. When critical longings for relationship with others and activity that makes a difference are frustrated, I experience more than manageable discomfort. I feel a deep sorrow, an *immobilizing lostness* that, at least for a time, empties my soul of energy to continue. But time and other experiences seem to help. Not always, but often. I begin to sense the return of movement toward life, the capacity to enjoy earlier pleasures and to press on with responsibilities. The color comes back into life, perhaps not richly, but enough to brighten the gray.

The third category of longings is an entirely different matter. Both critical longings and crucial longings involve desires for relationship and impact. But I long for a quality of relationship and a level of impact that no human being can ever provide. I was built for infinite love from Someone who needs nothing in return and for eternal impact through Someone whose purposes are supremely important. Only God can supply what my soul most deeply desires. When crucial longings are not satisfied, there is a pain that must be dealt with. Time will not help, except as it gives opportunity for denial and escape. In moments of deep pain, most encouragements and pleasures mean no more than a bucket of sand to a thirsty traveler. Life is slipping away, not just in neurotic perception, but in fact. Without Someone who cares and something to do that matters, life is an unspeakably cruel experience to be avoided, distorted, or denied. The consequence of living with no satisfaction of our crucial longings is the beginning of hell.

Looking for Fulfillment

When Christ promised to fill us with living water, He was obviously thinking of the satisfaction He yearns to provide for thirsty people. It is less clear exactly what thirsts He intends to satisfy, how He plans to satisfy them, and when we can hope to feel the effects of His provision.

To better understand the relationship of Christ's promise of living water to thirsty people, it will be helpful to sketch each category of longing as a circle and to arrange them concentrically as shown on the following page.

We spend our days most clearly aware of our least important longings and, as a result, are concerned more with their satisfaction

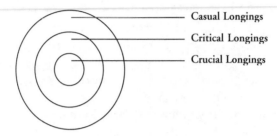

than with the others. We expend a fair amount of energy in arranging for our comfort. When the meal is tasty and the chest x-ray is clear, we feel good. Let the pleasant experience of satisfied casual longings be represented as a full outer circle.

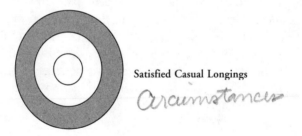

Satisfied Casual Longings

Circumstances

Most of us are in touch with critical longings as well, especially during periods of tension in our relationships. We feel angry and betrayed when spouses are cold, we hurt when friends are thoughtless. But when our primary relationships appear to be warm and healthy, the world can be a rather pleasant place to live. We sing of God's goodness with warmth and sincerity, we laugh easily at jokes, we look forward to an evening with old friends. We really feel quite good. If our casual longings remain unmet, we may feel intense discomfort but, at a "deeper level," we sense things are okay if our critical longings are satisfied. Let this experience be sketched this way:

Satisfied Critical Longings

Relationships

A few devoted Christians know what it means to taste the reality of God's presence when life is crumbling around them. Physical comforts may be few and friends may be insensitive and distant, but Christ somehow moves with sweetness and strength into the depths of their souls. "All that thrills my soul is Jesus" is the testimony of a special group of people whose lives are mysteriously attractive in the midst of suffering. These folks look like this:

Satisfied Crucial Longings

Communion w/ God

I think this sketch is more often claimed than experienced. Fullness in the outer two circles is often mistaken for the inexpressible joy of knowing the Lord. Enjoying the sought after *blessings* of God is sometimes confused with enjoying His *Person*.

It is entirely normal to fervently wish for fullness in all three circles: pleasant circumstances, strong relationships, and communion with God. And that is precisely the Christian's hope. The question to be asked has to do not with the eventual certainty of perfect happiness but rather with its timing and development.

There seem to be two broad ideas about the path to joy. One holds that God fills the circles of desire from the outside in. First He makes us comfortable. We trust Him for health and wealth. Then, as that develops, our relationships improve. Our marriages are strengthened, we learn to enjoy our money, sexuality, and personality as we relate to others similarly blessed. Then together, as a community of fulfilled and happy people, we praise God for His goodness. His blessings lead us more fully into His presence. This is a popular view, but one that, as I understand Scripture, reliably leads people away from maturity.

The second idea presents the process quite differently, contending that the deepest fullness comes during times of difficult struggle with denied comfort and strained relationships. Knowledge of God develops from the inside out. The two contrasting paths can be easily diagramed as shown on the following page.

The Painful Path to God

The sketches do not, of course, represent all the possibilities of either path. Rather, they highlight something essential about each. The second path, which I understand to better reflect the true nature of spiritual growth, assumes a key principle: *Until we acknowledge painful disappointment in our circumstances and relationships (particularly the latter), we will not pursue Christ with the passion of deep thirst. Or, to put it more simply, we rarely learn to meaningfully depend on God when our lives are comfortable.*

The promise of refreshing springs within us guarantees only that, for now, Christ will do something about our crucial longings.[1] We have no promise that He'll provide us with the comforts of health, prosperity, or leisure, nor can we depend on God to make our human relationships as warmly satisfying as we wish. His promise of daily bread and His pledge to supply us with what we need according to His riches must be carefully understood to mean that we can count on receiving from God all that's necessary to achieve His purpose in our life.

This kind of promise obviously does not guarantee us pain-free living on every level. On the contrary, because His intention

Path 1

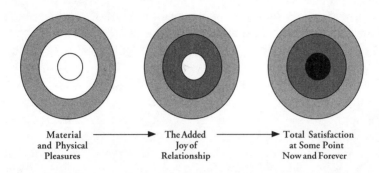

Material   The Added   Total Satisfaction
and Physical →   Joy of   →   at Some Point
Pleasures   Relationship   Now and Forever

Path 2

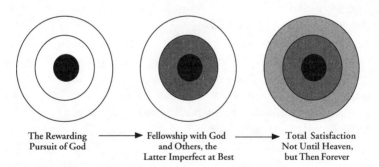

The Rewarding   Fellowship with God   Total Satisfaction
Pursuit of God → and Others, the   →   Not Until Heaven,
                  Latter Imperfect at Best but Then Forever

is to draw us deeply to Himself, and because we were designed to enjoy what only God can provide, we must honestly admit to deep sadness and disappointment, sometimes reaching the level of soul-wrenching despair, as we contemplate our human relationships. What we want simply is not there, but, as a fallen being, we naturally seek joy in every relationship except in our relationship with God. The result is inevitable frustration in our deepest parts. That frustration, properly handled, can drive us toward God.

Those who walk closest to God feel their disappointment most keenly. The awareness of *how things should be* (and one day will be) makes the reality of *how things are* all the more ugly. No matter how richly we experience the Lord, we cannot avoid the impact of living in a fallen world as a fallen being. Neither could our Lord. He was in perfect communion with the Father yet was still a man of sorrows, gripped to the point of tears by the hardness of men's hearts.

We simply must get rid of the idea that the obedient Christian is supposed to feel good all the time. The springs of living water bathing our deepest longings with His presence now and with His promises for later do not eliminate the pain of unmet desires at other levels. We therefore should not measure the quality of our walk with the Lord by the absence of unhappy feelings. When children rebel, parental pain is not only normal and real, it's healthy. And spiritual depth only intensifies the pain because it more keenly discerns how tragic rebellion is.

In spite of life's inevitable pain, it's possible to remain intact no matter what troubles crash into our life, because nothing can rob us of God's love—the very thing a self-aware, discerning soul wants the most. To be changed from the inside out means to learn how to drink from the living water of God's unchanging love so our purpose, identity, and joy give us the courage to respond well whether our life is smooth or rocky.

Imagine having such a clear vision of Christ that you could go to the stake with transcendent peace. Some people have actually done it. Picture what it would be like to look back on cruel mistreatment, perhaps sexual abuse, while looking forward to intimate relationships with confidence. It's rare, but it's possible.

Honest people touch the inevitable distress of life, sometimes through physical suffering, always through relational disappointment. Changed people taste the goodness of God so deeply that they pursue Him when life offers the legitimate but blander taste of nice homes, good health, and rich relationships—and they pursue Him all the more when those joys are removed.

Let me summarize.

1. We are thirsty people. We long for:
   a. physical comfort (casual longings);
   b. good relationships with people (critical longings);
   c. the joys that only relationship with God provides (crucial longings).
2. Christ has not promised to meet either our casual or critical longings. We may therefore bump into some hard times with material problems and unrewarding relationships. The promise in Matthew 6:25-34 must be interpreted to mean that God will faithfully provide all we need to accomplish His purpose in us and through us. There is no promise He'll give us all our purposes of immediate comfort would require.
3. He has promised to satisfy our crucial longings but:
   a. the satisfaction available now is only a taste. The banquet comes later. We will still ache, therefore, for more than what we have.
   b. the satisfaction of crucial longings does not dull the pain of disappointment when our casual and critical longings go unmet.
4. Disappointment is a chronic reality for the self-aware Christian, for at least three reasons:
   a. The complete joys of God will not be ours until heaven.
   b. No relationship on earth is perfect. We will, therefore, be disappointed in our critical longings.
   c. Fallen people naturally (but wrongly) depend on sources other than God (money, well-behaved children, warm churches, loving mates, successful careers) for satisfaction of their crucial longings. In so doing, they add to their necessary groaning the acute pain of frustrated demands (for example, "You must not leave me!") which creates bitterness, fear, self-reproach, and depression.

The longings of our heart must be faced. The disappointment of our soul must be experienced. Only then will we learn to pant after God in eager anticipation of His coming, when every desire will be forever satisfied. And only then will we learn how to free ourselves from self-centered preoccupation with the frustration of our longings so that real love of God and others becomes possible. Learning to enter into the disappointing realities of life is the focus of our next chapter.

NOTES

1. It should be noted that the facts about our relationship with Christ and the reality of that relationship from His perspective provide rich satisfaction of our deepest longings. Complete satisfaction in our present experience is hindered by two problems. First, we enjoy the presence of Christ by faith. The reality of face-to-face experience won't come until later. Second, our faith is imperfect. The wonder of "Christ in us" is muted by our dim apprehension of all He is. Therefore, even in the core of our being, satisfaction is far less now than it will be in heaven.

CHAPTER SIX

BECOMING AWARE OF OUR THIRST

Most of us cope with life by pretending. We pretend that what we have satisfies more than it does. And we pretend we haven't been hurt as badly as we have. The biblical instruction not to complain is more easily obeyed when we refuse to face what is disappointing and painful in our life. And yet I'm suggesting we take a look at precisely those things about life that may provoke complaint.

"But isn't it right," some say, "to give thanks in everything, to rejoice always, to press on as good soldiers of Jesus Christ?" An introspective look at our troubles seems inconsistent with all we should do. Why bother with a gloomy focus on those desires in our lives that remain unmet? It sounds so negative. Shouldn't we just get on with living?

In many Christian circles, maintaining a comfortable distance from inside problems is strongly encouraged. When teenagers struggle with resentment toward their parents or confusion about their identity, youth workers sometimes recommend more time in Bible study or renewed commitment to obedience. Both suggestions are good, but far too often hard questions get buried beneath a pile of memorized verses and stricter conformity to local standards of Christian conduct. The tough issues seem resolved when in fact they're merely shoved out of sight. They continue to take their toll on the teen's well-being, but now subtly rather than overtly. Sometimes the pastoral encouragement to be a better Christian protects the pastor from having to grapple with threatening concerns more than it gives the bewildered teenager clear direction for living.

A similar situation exists among women struggling with memories of sexual abuse. The intense feelings of shame and guilt that continue to overwhelm the victim for years after the abuse ended are far easier to suppress than to face. The longing to be held by someone who tenderly loves rather than selfishly exploits is deep, but often denied. It just hurts too much to admit what is wanted so badly when there's no guarantee of its availability.

There is incredible resistance—more in Christian circles, I think, than in secular—to owning internal pain. Even a glance in the direction of discouragement and fear violates our idea of what a victorious Christian should be doing. Many people have been trained in conservative churches and Christian families to deny that they hurt. Very few times have we been asked, with penetrating, sincere interest, how we really feel. A response longer than "Fine, thanks" is usually inappropriate. And we must admit *our* questions of others rarely invite a complete and honest sharing from their hearts. We all have a tendency to keep safely distant from each other's feelings. To deal with what's really going on inside is disturbing, too uncomfortable; so we hide the inside truth from others—and from ourselves. Life works better that way. That's the clear message we've learned from many of our teachers and the one we communicate to others by our non-involvement.

The difficulty with this teaching is that it's nearly true. It's right to be absorbed with the beauty of Christ and with our opportunities for worship and service. A focus on the heartaches of life can be grim business, leaving us cynical, depressed, and unmotivated. That's a clear danger of an inside look. Even if we grant that facing our emptiness is a necessary preliminary to trust, it's still true that entering into the reality of unmet longings is a painful process. And pain disrupts life. It can rob us of sleep; it sometimes triggers harsh responses to people we love; it tends to drive us toward immediate relief and away from responsibility. When I feel bad, I'm more tempted to watch television than to help my wife with housework.

Many Christians manage to keep life moving along rather smoothly without ever looking deeply at the pain in their souls. And the ones who do take a look sometimes crumble under the weight of what they discover. Why, then, take an inside look? If all it achieves is a greater awareness of unbelievable sorrow, why bother? Isn't it cruel to remind a desert traveler how parched his throat feels? Yes. If the only effect of becoming aware of our thirst is to heighten our misery, then it's stupid and wrong to look inside. On the other hand, if an awareness of our thirst is the beginning of closer fellowship with God (at whose right hand are abundant pleasures), then it makes sense. It is worth whatever temporary pain is stirred up, no matter how untemporary or severe the pain might seem.

The choice before us is rather stark: either live to be comfortable (both internally and externally, but especially internally) or live to know God. We can't have it both ways. One choice excludes the other.

In this chapter, I want to discuss why an awareness of thirst is the unavoidable first step toward real change—the kind that makes us more like Christ—and then to suggest what is required to experience the pain of unmet desires.

Why Should I Face My Thirst?

It hurts to experience the depths of an unsatisfied soul. So why do it? I want to suggest three reasons why feeling the pain of thirst is a necessary step toward changing from the inside out.

> ➤ Reason 1
>   Freedom from compulsive sin requires an awareness
>   of deep thirst.
> ➤ Reason 2
>   Sin will be understood superficially—and therefore
>   dealt with ineffectively—without an awareness of
>   deep thirst.

> Reason 3
> Without an awareness of deep thirst, our pursuit of
> God will be disciplined at best. With it, our pursuit
> can be passionate.

Reason 1: Freedom from Compulsive Sin

So many of us struggle with habits we can't seem to break, habits of thought as well as habits of deed. Some struggle with sexual fantasies that flood their minds, negativism toward every preacher they hear, contrived cheerfulness; others struggle with more obvious problems like masturbation, overeating, uncontrollable temper, crying spells, angry thoughts, laziness. Guilt-ridden Christians plead with God for help, but sleepless nights filled with sobbing prayers for strength to overcome fail to help. The habit continues to be the master. Why? Why do sincere effort, tearful repentance and promises to obey sometimes accomplish so little? What can be done?

Two interesting passages shed light on these difficult questions. In Romans 16:18 and Philippians 3:19, Paul speaks of people whose god is their appetite. The word for appetite in both texts is the same word used in John 7:38 to refer to that deep part within us that only Christ can fill, the part filled with what I've called our crucial longings. The teaching seems to be that people who don't know what it means to depend on Christ to satisfy their inmost being will experience an ache in their souls that relentlessly drives them toward immediate relief.

Casual longings, when frustrated, generate manageable discomfort. Unmet critical longings can lead to terrible heartache and a crushing sense of loss. But when crucial longings remain untouched, the very foundation of life crumbles. Without meaning in what I do or without love in my relationships, life simply isn't worth living.[1] The pain of aloneness and pointlessness is piercing. It *demands* relief.

That single fact—that the pain of living apart from God is unbearable—exposes our sinfulness as horribly grotesque and foolish. We insist on finding relief without coming to God *on His terms*. Many of us who are thirsty come to Christ for water—in fervent prayer, renewed commitment, and zealous service—but motivating our appeal is a demand for relief rather than a determination, come what may, to believe, to hope, and to love. When God does not accede to our demands, our only recourse is to handle the pain on our own. We must somehow remove ourselves from contact with the dreadful ache that continues to throb in our soul—the fear that we're unwanted and useless. Our only option is to use the resources under our control to numb our pain. We're limited to either denying how badly we hurt or to medicating ourselves through some form of temporary gratification.

One thing that seems clear is that movement toward pain is suicide. *But exactly the opposite is true!* The fact that the path to life often feels like the path to death, and that the path to death can feel like the path to life, is a tragic commentary on how far we have gotten off track. The process of becoming aware of our thirst is terrible. It hurts. It feels like the path to death. And once the process leads us beside the still waters, it starts all over as we are jerked from the grassy shore to the valley of trouble once again. But to explore and embrace our deepest hurts puts us in a small company of thirsty people who, *because they feel their thirst,* know what it means to come to Christ in deep and quiet trust.

It is important to realize that deadening the pain of unmet longings does not make them go away. The ache simply goes underground where it can't be dealt with effectively while it continues to press for relief with increased, and more subtle, urgency. The person who manages to deny his pain behind a facade of togetherness is dangerously vulnerable to developing compulsively sinful habits because he's not dealing a deathblow to the wrong strategies that block his enjoyment of the Lord. The unrecognized and largely unfelt ache in his soul still demands relief. He's ripe for being hooked when he stumbles onto something that provides a flash of excitement and a sense of fulfillment. The momentary relief of that core ache more closely resembles the experience of joyful living than anything he's known. It brings him closer than all his efforts to be obedient ever have.

Consider how an addiction to pornography might develop. A young Christian man with no history of sexual misbehavior spends an overnight visit with friends who have cable TV in the guestroom. As he prepares for bed, he flips on the television hoping to catch the late-night sports wrap-up. The TV is already set on a cable movie channel. The first picture to greet his eyes is a sexually explicit scene from an R-rated movie. Something stirs inside as his eyes fasten on the screen. More than the obvious arousal is involved. He feels something far deeper than sexual excitement; he feels alive and vital.

Some people in the same situation would immediately switch channels, believing it wrong to expose themselves to such stimulation. Others would watch it, enjoy it without that same sense of coming alive, turn it off when it was over, and think very little about what they saw.

Those who change channels quickly (a wise and right choice in my view) may do so out of a rigid adherence to moral standards that could be a response more to culture than to God. Certainly there are some who would reject the deceitful pull of the stimulation, recognizing that the promise of pleasure is real, but that the thrill runs shallow, endures for only a moment, and may carry a high price tag. These folks live with an awareness of deep longings they know sexual pleasures can only numb but never satisfy, and therefore, they consciously refuse spurious fulfillment in favor of what only God makes available. Although sexual stimulation can provide exciting satisfaction that seems to run far deeper than it does, the self-aware person knows his heart longs for something very different.

Assume the young man in the guestroom is a typical good Christian. He's sincerely committed to living for God and, as many churches would define the term, he's walking in fellowship with the Lord. But he's never faced the thirst of his soul. The profound disappointment of an uninvolved father has been written off as just one of those things. "Dad was gone a lot but I think I got used to it. It didn't bother me much. Dad loved me in his own way." Neither has the demeaning over-protection of a hovering mother been permitted to disturb him. "Mom? Oh, she's okay. Yeah, she bugs me some. I think she still wishes I was her little boy, but she means well. We get along fine."

Can you hear the denial of hurt in his words? He longs for a strongly involved father and a warmly accepting mother as any normal person does, but he dismisses the reality of a distant father and possessive mother as "no big deal." Why is it so hard to be honest about the disappointment we feel when others let us down? Why do we hide our disappointment behind claims of loyalty, respect, or strength? Can we not honor parents who frustrate us? To face that key people on whom we depend have not come through surfaces a level of pain that threatens to undo us. It seems as if the deepest longings of our heart are denied a response—and that feels like death. Better to stay away from the pain.

Perhaps the young man's apparent denial of disappointment is maturity, a recognition that nothing can shake him because he is loved by God. If that's true, then he would speak of our Lord with a quiet sense of reality that reflects a relationship of unusual depth. And he could fully acknowledge the legitimate suffering occasioned by insensitive parents without compromising his genuine love and appreciation for them. When the imperfections of another are realistically admitted, true love has its finest opportunity. Overlooking someone's faults is a different matter than pretending they have no faults. When we love people whose imperfections we're unwilling to face, our love is corrupted by self-protection. We need them to be more than they are. But when we fully admit their flaws, then our love can be truly accepting and directed at their welfare. To die for a friend is commendable. But to die for an enemy is the supreme example of love.

This man's love for his parents and for God does not reflect the warm strength of a mature believer. And he would not claim a high level of spiritual maturity. Sometimes in late-night chats with old friends from Bible college days, he wonders if the Christian life should spark more fire than what he knows burns in his soul. He admits to boredom, but keeps plugging away in the strength of conviction, habit, and social expectations.

And life is really quite pleasant. His casual desires are nicely met through a good job and excellent health. Plenty of friends—a few he considers close—prevent his critical longings from provoking severe discomfort. With the optimism reserved for younger folks, he assumes he will one day meet the "right woman" and will become a well-established, happy, and prosperous family man.

Crucial longings for involvement with God present no conscious problem; he is respected as a committed evangelical. Only rarely does he sense a need for deepened fellowship with Christ. Thoughts of a bolder, more passionate life with Christ are dismissed as the concern of older believers and struggling missionaries.

A few problems disrupt the pleasantness of life—only a few, none serious. Occasional bouts with temper bother him a bit. And a habit of saying yes to responsibilities at church he would rather not accept generates some time pressures. Masturbation has been a problem, especially during teen years. Less now. Regular devotions, more exercise, and prayerful determination have helped him keep the habit under nearly perfect control.

Very few would pick this man as a candidate for developing a serious compulsion for pornography. Why did a five-second scene of explicit sexual behavior produce a sense of satisfaction so rich that it seemed necessary for life? Why was his mind flooded for hours, days, even weeks with images of what he'd seen on TV? Why during his next trip to the quick-stop food store did he linger by the magazine rack? Why did he soon create a reason to pay a second visit to his friend who has cable TV? Why did he sign up for cable himself three months later, persuading himself that he only wanted better reception and access to the twenty-four-hour-a-day sports channel?

Four years after that stay in his friend's guest room he came to me with an obsessive preoccupation with pornography. He sneaked into adult bookstores, stayed up late at night to watch sexually explicit movies, and couldn't look at an attractive woman without mentally undressing her. Why? What happened?

The problem is more easily explained than solved, but even the explanation requires careful thought. The principle to understand is this: *Most habits that we seem powerless to control grow out of our attempts to relieve the unbearable tension that results from our failure to deal with the disappointment of our deepest longings for relationship.* This young man was hooked on pornography because the thrill of sexual pleasure more closely approximated the genuine joys of deep relationship than any experience he had known. Living with shallow relationships is risky. Unless we are moving toward other folks with the love with which God moved toward us, the appeal of a broad range of intense pleasures may become compulsively attractive.

The power of bad habits is not simply in the pleasure they provide. Sinful habits become compulsively attractive when the pleasure they give relieves deep disappointment in the soul better than anything else one can imagine.[2] The good feelings offered by having enjoyable sex, eating delicious food, or controlling crowds with skilled oratory can numb the ache of unmet longings by providing a satisfaction that, for a time, fulfills like nothing else ever has. People feel alive in the midst of consuming pleasure. Thus, whatever generates the pleasure seems so right. Pleasures of the body (such as sex or eating) and of the mind (such as power or applause) can be marvelous counterfeits of real life, when God has not been tasted. Their insidious appeal lies in their power to give quick relief from groaning, relief that feels more than good—it feels like life.

When pleasures of any kind are used to satisfy (or at least to quiet) our crucial longings, then the craving for what only God can provide becomes a demanding tyrant driving us toward whatever relief is available. Our god becomes our appetite. Crucial longings meant to create a panting after God energize our addiction to whatever feels good for a moment. How tragic!

"If anyone is thirsty, let him come to *me* and drink." Each of us is thirsty, but few understand and deeply experience the pain of it. Those who do, however, are better equipped to recognize the deceitful allure of lesser pleasures and then to resist opportunities that falsely promise a taste of wholeness. Those who refuse to honestly face their disappointments and hurts (people like the young man addicted to pornography) are more vulnerable to the devilish power of shallow fun to masquerade as an angel of life.

Reason 2: More Than a Superficial Understanding of Sin

Consider a second reason why Christians do well to admit the painfulness of unsatisfied thirst. Without an appreciation and acceptance of what we long for, our ability to love will be limited by a failure to recognize the ways in which we violate love to protect ourselves from personal pain. Think with me about the relationship between admitting our unsatisfied longings and recognizing the subtle sin of self-protection.

Some folks manage quite well to resist temptation to obvious sin without ever becoming aware of their thirst. And that, of course, is commendable. Resisting sin is always the right thing to do. But for someone out of touch with his thirst, the source of the strength required to avoid obvious sin is usually some combination of self-discipline, time in Scripture and prayer, support and expectations from a community of Christian friends, a healthy concern for the consequences of moral lapse, and a sincere commitment to behave as God commands. The result of living in dependence upon the elements in this impressive list is (at best) a blameless life characterized by high standards, sacrificial commitment, tireless service, and rigidity. When Christians honor their lofty calling without passionately experiencing and embracing the deep ache in their souls, something important, even vital, is lost. Their approach to people is less human, less real, less "there." Often they instruct, motivate, and challenge others, but their lives fail to draw people to the Lord. They push more than entice.

Unfeigned love, something hard to define but unmistakable in its impact, can spring only from the deepest parts of our soul. That part of us that longs to be loved and keenly feels every disappointment is the only part of our being from which we can richly love others, including God. To look away from profound disappointment requires that we lose touch with the liveliest part of who we are. Protection against pain blunts our capacity to love.

When our approach to life revolves around discipline, commitment, and knowledge but runs from feeling the hurt of unmet longings, then our efforts to love will be marked more by required action than by liberating passion. We will be known as reliable, but not involved. Honest friends will report that they enjoy being with us, but have trouble feeling close. Even our best friends (including spouses) will feel guarded around us, a little tense and vaguely distant. It's not uncommon for Christian leaders to have no real friends.[3]

This is indeed a sad state of affairs, one that leaves many people (including leaders) unnecessarily lonely and therefore prone to burnout or illegitimate intimacy. But worse, a person who denies his deepest disappointments relates to others in a fashion corrupted by unrecognized but serious sin. When the thirsts of our soul are neither understood nor embraced, love is violated in many ways that typically go unnoticed and therefore unresolved. Let me explain.

Paul instructs us to look on the interests of others as greater than our own. Clearly the dividing line between a life lived in the flesh and one empowered by the Spirit is self- versus other-centeredness. There is one source of energy behind every interpersonal act: either a priority interest in ourselves or a priority interest in others. The mark of the Christian is a quality of love that directs more energy toward others' concerns than toward one's own well-being. Nominal Christians and unbelievers are capable of extraordinary acts of kindness, but only the trusting Christian can be concerned with another's longings more than with his own. Unfortunately, however, very few are. The church has lost its power because it loves so poorly.

Consider this idea: *Whenever we're motivated more by concern for self than by concern for others, we're working to dull the impact of our disappointed longings.* I've already suggested that our deepest longings, the ones that must be satisfied if life is to be worth living, will not be fully met until heaven. Happiness is rooted more in hope than in present experience. Life as we know it in a fallen world requires that we experience an unrelieved ache in our soul, an ache that can explode into searing pain when aggravated by others. Unkind words from a friend, a snub by an officemate, or a sullen mood in a child can sometimes trigger a reaction far more intense than the injury warrants. Why? Perhaps the disturbing event pushed us closer to the chronic pain within, the ache of profound disappointment we desperately deny. We're left with the choice to run from the ache and wrap ourselves in self-protection or to embrace the ache and rest secure in our Lord's promise: "Do not let your hearts be troubled … If I go and prepare a place for you, I will come back and take you to be with me that you also may be where I am" (John 14:1,3). Self-protection or trust: Every behavior ultimately reflects one choice or the other. We either accept groaning as a way of life and eagerly await our Lord's return with single-minded devotion to Him, or we try to escape the unpleasantness of a groaning heart by denying the impact of any troubling reminder that life is not as it should be.

The latter option is the sin of self-protection. It stains our best efforts to love, shaping our style of relating to fit defensive purposes. Much of our polite conversation and pleasant fellowship is little more than two protective styles of relating that comfortably mesh. Many husbands and wives spend whole lifetimes keeping their distance from each other and on their golden anniversary celebrate a durable but passionless partnership.

Our insulating layers of friendliness and appropriate involvement work to keep us from touching the terrible pain of previously felt disappointment. We have all been let down, and it hurt. Our commitment is to never hurt like that again. We therefore try to love from a distance. But it can't be done. We try anyway, because maintaining distance from our pain is more important to us than reaching true closeness to God and others.

Men who as boys felt neglected by their dads often remain distant from their children. The sins of fathers are passed on to children, often through the dynamic of self-protection. It hurts to be neglected, and it creates questions about our value to others. So to avoid feeling the sting of further rejection, we refuse to give that part of ourselves we fear might once again be received with indifference.

Self-protective disengagement can take many forms. Some fathers work too hard; they feel more adequate in their jobs than at home. Others involve themselves in every family activity that presents itself. Some dads never miss their sons' ball games, they spend weekends on family outings, they read bedtime stories to sleepy children. But their motive for impressive involvement can still be self-protection. Some men move toward their families in a desperate (and demanding) attempt to win the involvement they never had from their own parents. Again, self-protection, not love.

In Part Three of this book, I more thoroughly discuss the nature of self-protective sin. The subject deserves extended treatment because self-protection is the silent killer of true community. Like untreated high blood pressure, it is rarely recognized but it drains the health and life out of relationships.

Our Lord Jesus taught that in the day when we Christians are judged He'll take a look inside each of us to see what was beneath our actions. The kind deeds that were prompted by self-protection and not by genuine love will be burned up in the pile with lies, temper explosions, and sexual sins. Self-protection is subtle but serious because it motivates so much of how we behave with each other. Friendliness can protect us from rejection. Humor can help us avoid isolation. A businesslike efficiency can keep people away from a tenderness that might be exploited. Shyness might be the means to keep us from ever looking foolish.

Certainly there are folks who are friendly, funny, businesslike, or shy for reasons other than self-protection. It's fair (though not terribly scientific) to say that people are sometimes "that way" because of natural, inherent personality tendencies. But we too often explain away self-protective motivation by shrugging our shoulders and saying, "Well, that's just the way I am. That's my temperament, I guess."

We will not recognize the subtle sin of self-protection until we realize the pain from which we want to protect ourselves. And that's the key point I want to make for now. If the thirst of our soul is neither understood nor experienced, we won't be inclined to ask whether our style of relating to people could be designed to keep us safely out of touch with the pain of a relentless thirst. To deeply understand sin—the ways in which we violate love—we must first become aware of our thirst. Facing disappointment is necessary for Christian growth.

Reason 3: The Passionate Pursuit of God

I have long been puzzled by the number of people I know whose apparently sincere commitment to Christianity lacks a passion for Christ. One would think that when a thirsty desert traveler spots an oasis, he feels some excitement as he drags his weary body across the burning sand toward the cool springs.

Perhaps that's the problem. How many of us see ourselves as desperately thirsty people who see only sand or Christ? When I'm not thirsty, a tall glass of water has little appeal. When I don't feel the longings of my heart, then the eagerness I sense about Christ extends no further than my hope for physical comfort and fulfilling relationships (what I hope He'll do for my casual and critical longings). With that sort of thinking, there is none of the passion of intimacy between the Lord Jesus and me. Men whose biblical scholarship and involvement in Christian duties put me to shame sometimes speak of their relationship to God as others might discuss their loyalty to a company that treats them well. Others talk about Christianity as a system of thought that explains things for them. The idea of an eager Bridegroom entering His bride to produce His fruit in her is lost in a Christianity that majors on propositions and overlooks the longings of the heart (which the propositions tell us Jesus can meet!).

For years, the church has divided over a *solid faith* rooted in propositional truth versus an *exciting faith* drawn from our experience of Christ. Charismatics in the church seem to offer vibrancy to bored Christians, while conservative noncharismatics call us back to the Word—studied, learned, and obeyed. The former run the risks of subjectivism, such as measuring the truthfulness of a teaching by its felt impact rather than by its biblical support and, in the process, slighting the "unexciting" truths of Scripture. The latter slip too often into the ugliness of cold orthodoxy, forgetting that the truth of God is designed to invade every part of a person's life, bringing him into rich involvement with Christ and others.

Perhaps the missing element in both camps is the neglect of an important doctrine of Scripture, namely man's dependency on God. We are quick to acknowledge we all need God. But for what? Salvation, certainly, and for instruction and the strength to follow it. But isn't there more? What of the thirst passages? The passion of the panting psalmist is rarely explored as reflecting the core of man's dependency. We cannot live without God because we were built to enjoy what only He provides. Our longings are therefore at the very center of our dependency.

The doctrine of depravity (which we will emphasize in Part Three) needs to be complemented with a clearer doctrine of dependency. We are not "getting psychological" when we talk of man's longings. The concept is thoroughly biblical. The phrase "cold orthodoxy" is a contradiction in terms. True orthodoxy is never cold; it is always hot-blooded and alive. When we add to our doctrinal positions an understanding of our longing, dependent, thirsty heart—and develop the courage to *feel* the reality of that teaching in our soul—then we can remain rooted in propositional revelation without sacrificing our passion.

So many sincere Christians remain steadfast in their faith week after week, year after year, wondering where the reality is. The missing key, I believe, is a recognition of the importance of good relationships throughout the Bible. The entire fabric of Scripture is woven with the thread of relationship. God longs for us to give our heart to Him. He loves us. To the degree that we embrace our thirst and realize who He is, we long for Him. There is nothing dull about the romance between our heavenly Bridegroom and His hurting but fickle bride. The more honestly we face whatever hurt may be locked inside, the more passionately we can be drawn to the beauty of a Lover who responds consistently with all the tender strength our heart desires.

People who stay away from their hurt tend to develop a matter-of-fact relationship with Christ. Their energy is released more in ideas, causes, or projects than in relationship. These are folks who may be affable, even thoughtful, but you rarely sense the force of their presence. They are not the ones who come to mind when tragedy strikes and you need a friend to be there.

Lonely people fill our churches. They attend Sunday school, chat socially at church dinners, and interact meaningfully in small group Bible studies. They often feel reasonably happy, enjoying whatever is pleasant and pressing on despite the rest. But there are moments, moments when a sense of emptiness pierces them like a sword. They may weep, then recover, and get on with life. When a Christian filled with passion speaks to them, they feel strangely stirred. A part of their soul that has lain dormant, sometimes for decades, is touched. A trickle of cool water runs down their throat, making them aware of how thirsty and parched they have been. Hope revives: Maybe life could be more than pleasant. Maybe it could *mean* something. Perhaps it's possible to feel deeply alive—struggling, sometimes severely—but *alive!*

People who embrace their hurt are able to pursue God more passionately. And their passion is contagious. Less passionate people can *instruct* others in biblical living, but only people filled with passion can *draw* others into biblical relationships.

In summary, understanding and experiencing thirst is necessary to:

> ➤ *break bad habits* without becoming mechanistically self-controlled and thereby losing the engaging warmth of humanness;
> ➤ *recognize subtle sin,* the many ways in which we violate relationships through self-protection;
> ➤ *develop passion* in our pursuit of God, the kind of passion that can draw others into meaningful life in Christ.

How Do I Face My Thirst?

Becoming aware of our deepest longings is a painful process and therefore will not come easily. The recognition of an unfilled void, a vague sense of emptiness that can be temporarily suppressed but never resolved, can disturb an otherwise comfortable life or add to the difficulty of a life already distressed. We strongly prefer to admit only those problems we can handle: "You're struggling with anger? Okay, here's what to do." "Some tension in your marriage? Worry over finances? Follow this list of steps and your problems will be changed into blessings!"

Taking control of our life according to biblical principles often distances us from feeling the thirst that requires vulnerable trust and tough faith. It's right, of course, to assume responsibility in money matters (for example, budgeting, wise spending, generous giving, careful record-keeping), family issues (for example, communication, shared labor in the home, conflict resolution), and personal habits (for example, right eating, exercise, prayer, and Bible study). But no amount of responsibility-taking will ever relieve the thirst for relationship. Only heaven offers complete satisfaction. Until then, a disturbing sense of incompleteness will continue to blemish the most responsible and most blessed life. We can deny it, we can cover it over with busyness and pleasures, but we cannot get rid of it.

We have discussed the importance of tasting the reality of our inevitable disappointment with life. But how do we do it? How do we feel a thirst that so many elements in life combine to deny? The how-to's of acknowledging thirst might be organized into three suggestions:

1. Ask the tough questions that produce *confusion*.

2. Explore the imperfections of key relationships until you experience deep *disappointment*.

3. Study your own approach to relationships with an openness to developing *conviction*.

First, Ask the Tough Questions That Produce Confusion.

God tells us enough to establish, direct, and nourish our faith, but He doesn't tell us enough to end confusion. What He does and what He allows can sometimes be baffling, even maddening.

For example, newly converted parents decided to enroll their thirteen-year-old daughter in a Christian school in an effort to promote the values and standards they now embraced. One of the girl's teachers in the new school introduced her to drugs. She went on to develop a major drug abuse problem that continued through most of her teen years. The family was thrown into chaos. Several years of residential treatment were required before light appeared at the end of the tunnel.

The girl's parents did not make their decision lightly when they sent her to the Christian school. Considerable prayer, advice from several pastors, and a thorough research of the school all were involved in the move. Their question of me has been repeated countless times by others whose lives, through no fault of their own, have come apart: "Why did God let this happen?"

The tendency in most of us is to look for a way to wrap the painful question in pretty paper. We want to provide an answer that settles things on a positive note, or, when that seems out of reach, at least closes down an uncomfortable discussion.

There are biblical truths that deal with the tough questions. God's demonstration of love at the Cross should end all doubt as to whether God is for us. The fact of His sovereignty requires us to finally be still. But when legitimate truth is offered for the purpose of shutting down hard questions, that truth becomes a cliché. Sincere questions spoken from a heart of pain must be allowed to open the door to confusion. To slam the door shut, and in so doing to assert that honest confusion has no place in our pursuit of God, leads to a forced, mechanical trust rather than to a real and vital confidence.

Another strategy for avoiding confusion is to respond to a troubling situation with an exclusive focus on "what should be done about it." You work hard at providing your children with a good and godly home. You have wonderful expectations for how things will be as they mature. When one phone call brings all your hopes crashing down, you must handle a situation you never dreamed would come into your life. Your mind immediately grasps for solutions. And it's right to stand up and do what can be done rather than to crumble in a heap and stay there. In every situation, there's a way to respond that pleases God. And that must be our goal: to please God rather than to relieve all distress. But sometimes a strong determination to meet a tough problem head-on can grow out of a stronger desire to avoid the churning of unresolved confusion in our soul. It's frightening to feel that life is out of our control. But it's far better to spend a few sleepless nights in confused weeping than to become dispassionately efficient in our manner of relating.

Facing confusion honestly gives strong faith the opportunity to develop. When life makes no sense, when moments of absolute confusion shred our soul, there are only three things we can do: (1) We can abandon any claim to Christian belief and search for immediate relief and happiness (or, if that can't be found, we can commit suicide). (2) We can run from confusion as a woodsman would flee a hungry bear. A "Christian" strategy for ending confusion is to deny the reality of disturbing questions behind renewed commitment to the truth of God. Such a strategy produces rigid dogmatism, which saps our faith of its vitality. Legalism will not allow us to be troubled by exploring tough questions. Investigation is replaced entirely by indoctrination. (3) In the face of confusion we may choose to cling with disciplined tenacity to Christ, to who He is and to what He taught, even as our struggle with confusion continues unabated. The record of Habakkuk's life begins with a bewildered prophet who soon becomes even more upset by confusion. He did not become silent (chapter 2) until he fully entered and expressed his confusion. God then revealed Himself to His servant in a way that led Habakkuk to proclaim a confidence in God that no confusion could shake. That's the model.

Be open to looking at everything in your life. Don't run too quickly from disturbing events and insights into an affirmation of your faith that's more contrived than real. Let your mind explore the hard issues that provoke some really unsettling questions in order to provoke a more trusting awareness of Christ.

> ➤ The uncle who molested you when you were a little girl. He was a respected elder in your church. What on earth do you do with that? Suspect everyone's integrity?
> ➤ The move you made because of your job, a decision God seemed to clearly indicate, that robbed your kids of a great youth group in an alive church. You have now lived without a good church for several years. The youth group is so small and the rules so severe that you don't require your kids to attend, and now they're slipping away from the Lord. How do you fit all that together in your mind?
> ➤ The doctor you consulted who misdiagnosed your problem. Now you're permanently disabled from a problem that should have been recognized. Your doctor is a good one. He "just happened" to make a human error in your case. Do you just remind yourself of Romans 8:28 and go on? What do you do with your angry confusion?

Perhaps I've made my point: An honest look at life will produce confusion. But confusion isn't bad, it's good, because in the middle of confusion we become aware of a passionate desire to know that Someone strong and kind is working behind all we see, moving things carefully toward a just and joyful conclusion.

God does enlighten us on certain points. We must learn what He has revealed and believe all that's clear. But even the best-taught Bible student must throw up his hands at some point. There is a level of confusion that will not disappear, and we must accept that fact. As long as we think we can clear our confusion with more study and further research, we will not be driven to passionate faith. But when we admit that important parts of our life will continue to be clothed in confusion, then we can learn to relax in our faith in God. Tough faith never grows in a comfortable mind. But it can develop nicely when our mind is so troubled by confusion that we either believe God or give up on life. *Letting ourselves experience confusion creates a thirst that only faith can satisfy.*

Second, Explore the Imperfections of Key Relationships Until You Experience Deep Disappointment.

Remember our purpose. We want to learn what it means to pant after God, to come to Jesus as thirsty people. Only thirsty people pant. Because we're skilled at denying the thirst that exposes our dependency on God, we must discover how we can become aware of our deepest thirst. Facing confusion is one way. Feeling disappointment is another.

Perhaps the most difficult thing for many people to admit is that they feel let down by their parents. Even victims of child abuse sometimes cling to the hope that the abusing parent really loved them "but didn't know how to show it." It's hard to squarely face the fact that we have not been loved with the love we want so badly. It's been my experience in counseling that people more easily admit to their own failure to love others than to the profound disappointment a parent's love has been to them.

Many of us have wonderful parents, as I do, for whom we are deeply grateful. But all of us long for what the very best parent can never provide: perfect love that's always there with understanding, deeply and sacrificially concerned *at every moment* for our welfare, never too burdened with its own cares to be sensitive to ours, strong enough to handle a full awareness of our faults without retreating, and wise enough to direct us properly at every crossroad. No parent measures up to those standards, yet our heart will settle for nothing less. And because every child naturally turns to his primary caregiver for what he desperately wants, every child is disappointed.

To expect an exquisite meal from a decent restaurant will leave us disappointed with a pretty good dinner. To know the exquisite meal is coming later can help us gratefully accept the good food available now. And that's the point of facing our disappointment with parents and everyone else. We have looked to people for all we need. When we "try to love them" by covering over our disappointment with them, our love is built on denial. But when we acknowledge the deep ache in our soul *which would not be there* had our parents loved us perfectly, we begin to see how thirsty we are for what no one has provided. We can recognize our demanding dependence on people, our sinful insistence that others do for us what they cannot do (a form of idolatry). When we learn to accept people who disappoint us by no longer requiring them to satisfy us, then we're free to love them, to reach toward them for their sake without having to protect ourselves from feeling disappointed by their response to us.

Our Lord compressed the whole law into two commands: Love God and love others. The mature Christian is one who is growing in his ability to love people as they are, not as he wishes them to be. The purpose of admitting how disappointed we are in everyone else is not to fuel our criticism and anger or to fasten the blame for our failures on how our parents raised us. The purpose is precisely the opposite: to expose to ourselves how we wrongly demand that others always come through for us and to learn to move toward them without that demand, to love them freely and genuinely.

But there's a condition that must be met if the outcome of facing our disappointment is to be strengthened love rather than fueled resentment and self-pity. We must learn to hope. Feeling our disappointment puts us in touch with a part of our soul that longs for much more than anyone in this life will ever provide. As we ache over the reality of wanting what we do not have, we can begin to understand Paul's eager anticipation of the Lord Jesus' return. Keenly felt disappointment in the present supplies the energy for passionate hope for the future.

The hope of Christ's return has an effect on the lives of confidently waiting Christians. It purifies us (1 John 3:3). When we know that every longing of our heart will one day be eternally and completely satisfied, we learn to live without demanding anything now. Hope is the antidote for disappointment and the demandingness it creates. With confidence in the Lord, we are free to love, to risk more disappointment, to face the inevitability of frustration, to embrace that frustration as a stimulus to a more passionate hope. *Feeling disappointment puts us in touch with a thirst that only hope can satisfy.*

Third, Study Your Own Approach to Relationships with an Openness to Developing Conviction.

Much more will be said in Part Three about our sinful strategies for coping with unmet longings. For now, I want to make the simple point that facing our disappointment in others can lead not only to a passionate hope for heaven but also to a convicting awareness of how our style of relating to people is often more self-protective than it is loving.

One man confessed to a small support group of Christians that he'd patterned his approach to relationships after the Clint Eastwood image: tough, silent, impassive. He'd begun to see that what he called manliness was in fact a protection against vulnerable involvement. He was scared to talk openly with his wife for fear he'd be exposed as inadequate to deeply touch her.

Studying our style of relating can create a profound desire to love better. We were designed not only to be loved, but to love. As we face our failure to love and begin to see how so much of what we do is stained by a self-centered commitment to avoid hurting, the Spirit of God convicts us of our sinfulness. We can move on to a repentance that frees us to more fully enjoy God's love and to more freely love Him and others in return. "Search me, O God, and know my heart… See if there is any offensive way in me, and *lead me in the way everlasting*" (Psalm 139:23-24). *Praying for conviction produces a thirst for relating to others with a purer love.*

Confused? The answer is faith. Disappointed? Only hope will do. Convicted? Learn how to love. "And now these three remain: faith, hope and love. But the greatest of these is love" (1 Corinthians 13:13).

Facing confusion, feeling disappointment, and praying for conviction will deepen our awareness of how thirsty our soul really is. And then we will listen eagerly when our Lord says, "If anyone is thirsty, let him come to me." Let me summarize the reasons for facing our thirst:

1. It can free us from the enslaving power of those sins that deceitfully provide exciting, but temporary and costly, satisfaction.
2. It can deepen our awareness of how we fail others and thus lead to richer relationships.
3. It can increase our passion for pursuing God and make us effective in drawing others to Him.

The route to facing our thirst involves three key steps:
1. Admit confusion:
   - ➤ Ask tough questions.
   - ➤ Don't cover confusion with the blanket of dogmatism or easy answers.
   - ➤ Let confusion drive you to faith.
2. Acknowledge disappointment:
   - ➤ Reflect on how others have let you down or failed to come through as you deeply wanted them to.
   - ➤ Don't numb your disappointment with the anesthetic of denial, forced love, or cheap forgiveness.
   - ➤ Let disappointment drive you to hope.
3. Accept conviction:
   - ➤ Look squarely at how you protect yourself from feeling disappointment in relationships by

keeping your distance from people.
- ➤ Don't escape conviction by trying hard to always do the right thing. Explore the motives beneath your good behavior.
- ➤ Let conviction drive you to love.

Change from the inside out begins with an awareness of our thirst. It continues with an awareness of how we try to satisfy our thirst with our own resources.

How do we give up digging our own wells so we can turn to the well of living water? What does it mean to let the Lord quench our thirst? That is the subject of Part Three.

NOTES

1. It follows, happily, that when we learn to trust God for our crucial longings, we develop an intactness of identity and purpose that can be badly shaken but will never be destroyed by even the most severe frustration of lesser longings.

2. To have a parent or friend whose relationship to Christ is clearly real and strangely enticing gives a hope of joy that preserves us from the lure of sinful pleasures. As a child I watched with fascination as my dad prayed in church. His prayers were different from so many others. They were real. He seemed to believe he was really talking to someone. That made an enduring impression on me. I didn't want to settle for shallow pleasure when contact with God was possible. I could imagine reality because I tasted it in Dad's relationship with God.

3. Teachers of future Christian leaders, in an effort to warn against the dangers of favoritism and division, have sometimes advised their students to develop no close friends among the people they serve. Surely there must be a better solution to the potential for favoritism than this. That sort of advice violates not only the design of Christ's Body and strengthens the snobbish and self-serving division between clergy and laity, but it also requires people to deny their essential relational nature and thereby creates robot-like leaders instead of deeply involved servants.

PART THREE
DIGGING BROKEN WELLS

"Even when I get what I want, it's not what I want."

CHAPTER SEVEN

LOOKING IN ALL THE WRONG PLACES

"Are you willing to follow Christ?" The hundreds of teenagers shift uncomfortably in their seats as they hear the speaker boom out the challenge at the morning meeting.

"He invites you to come to Him, to really come, to come in total surrender. If you're sick and tired of playing at Christianity, then take His invitation seriously and come. Get your drugs, your porno magazines, your rock tapes—get everything that defiles you—and bring it all tonight to the rally. We'll have a great burning of all these tools of the Devil to symbolize your decision to follow Christ."

That night, dozens of kids, with eyes moist and jaws firmly set, dump their marijuana, *Penthouses*, and Bon Jovi tapes in a pile outside the meeting room. As the fire roars, they all join hands and sing, "I have decided to follow Jesus."

As a teen, I took part in similar happenings, making strong commitments as I stared into the dying campfire to never miss devotions and to witness every day. But although good spiritual directions were sometimes set in these moments, the promises I made on the mountaintop often dissolved into complacency when I returned to the valley of everyday life. Something inside me that needed to be dealt with was never touched.

I believe good things can happen when kids determine in their hearts to follow Christ. Any Christian parent would be thrilled to know his son or daughter—especially one whose lifestyle has caused so much worry—promised to stay away from illicit drugs and pornographic literature. And most would applaud a decision to no longer listen to rock music, if not from spiritual concern, then at least for auditory relief. That youth meeting has real value.

I would assume that of the young people who contributed to the pile of things to be burned, a fair number were making meaningful decisions in which the Holy Spirit had a hand. But I'm not at all persuaded that the youth speaker's message communicated an accurate understanding of what it means to come to Christ. The flight from lust, the avoidance of even the appearance of evil, and separation from the things of the world are all included in a serious commitment to Christ, but they are more the *fruit* of coming to Christ than the *core*. Certainly you cannot claim to be following Christ while at the same time stubbornly continuing in obvious sin. The *Penthouse* magazines should be burned.

But so much more is involved in changing from the inside out than pulling rotten fruit off the tree. Our struggle against sin requires a far tougher battle than the struggle to do right and not do wrong. When the battle is fought by trying hard to do all the Bible commands, eventual defeat is guaranteed. Either we'll slip into defeat and frustration or we'll become stiff and self-righteous in our disciplined conformity to standards, unable to relate deeply to anyone, including God.

The Bible speaks of wicked behavior as the outgrowth of a wicked and deceitful heart. The central problem is *inside*, within the heart. Effort will always be required to do what's right, but when we understand how to recognize and deal with *sin in the heart*, then the shift from sinful behavior to godly behavior will reflect an internal change that makes the shift real. As Jesus said, "First clean the inside of the cup and dish, and then the outside also will be clean" (Matthew 23:26).

But what does that mean? It's easier to understand change in behavior than change in the heart. I know when I do wrong things like cheating or smoking pot, but how can I know if my heart is improved? What's wrong with my heart anyhow? Isn't it enough to make an internal decision to follow Christ and then to demonstrate the reality of that decision by doing what is right? What did our Lord have in mind when He spoke about cleaning our insides?

A Clearer View of Sin

To more fully grasp our Lord's teaching we need a clearer understanding of sin, especially the sinfulness that stains our heart. For ease of discussion, divide the problem of sin into two categories: (1) *visible acts of transgression against clearly written biblical standards* and (2) *subtle violations of our Lord's command to love*. When the second category is poorly understood, people expend all their spiritual energy in carefully defining biblical standards and working hard to keep them. The usual result is pharasaical righteousness—or guilty frustration. Dealing only with the first category of sin will not lead to change from the inside out.

When we read that Moses "chose to be mistreated along with the people of God rather than to enjoy the pleasures of sin for a short time" (Hebrews 11:25), we tend to think of the worldly opportunities for pleasure available in Pharaoh's court that Moses gave up—opportunities for power, luxury, rich foods, and sensual comforts, to name a few. And that thinking is correct: Moses did turn his back on immediate comfort to pursue God's purposes. But when we apply that passage to our life today we usually end up with a list of things we shouldn't do. Egypt's pleasures must be abandoned. For teens those pleasures might include drugs, rock music, and a preoccupation with fashion. For adults, the list may prohibit drinking, materialism (often measured by an expensive car and a half-tithe), affairs, corporate climbing, and soap operas.

Different churches emphasize different evils, but most Christian communities have a code of conduct (written or unwritten) by which spirituality can be measured. More often than not, evangelical Christians who sincerely want to grow are preoccupied almost exclusively with sins in the first category, visible transgressions of easily recognized standards. The result of that preoccupation is a powerless church in which central problems are not dealt with and lives remain unchanged.

The focus is wrong. I have no argument with exhorting people to abandon clearly sinful practices and to develop good habits. Nor would I quarrel with holding people accountable within a loving community to live as they should. But a sharp focus on visible conformity to specific standards of right and wrong can easily lead to a disastrous neglect of subtle sins against relationship.

Our Lord severely rebuked the Pharisees for their scrupulous tithing, not because careful adherence to standards is wrong, but because they were neglecting *more important matters*, like justice, mercy, and faithfulness (Matthew 23:23), matters that pertain to the way people treat one another. The problem was not with their tithing, it was with their failure to deal with sins against relationship.

When our Lord invites thirsty people to come to Him, He intends for us to do more than burn our dirty magazines. He requires us to look carefully at our approach to relationships to see where self-interest corrupts love. The whole purpose of the law is to point the way toward quality relationships with God and others. To understand what the invitation to come entails, we must go beyond a legitimate concern with visible sin and explore the ways in which thirsty people who desperately want relationship foolishly violate the command to love.

We have already discussed the difficult truth that life is disappointing. No one comes through for us as we want them to, and God requires that we postpone complete satisfaction now (which isn't available anyway) and trust Him for a better day. But we don't like the wait. We hurt now and we want relief now. If God won't provide us the relief we demand, then we'll take matters into our own hands. As we move through life, trying to make a living, handling our responsibilities, planning fun times on weekends, and developing relationships that are both enjoyable and meaningful, we live out a deep commitment to minimize disappointment and pain. Because relationships have the most potential for pain, our commitment to self-protection is most strongly honored in the ways we approach people.

Change from the inside out requires that we look beneath the surface of life to see not only the deep longings of our thirsty soul but also the self-protective commitments of our deceitful heart. In Part Two we discussed our thirst. Part Three looks at our strategies for relating to imperfect people who let us down and to a God who responds to our pain with understanding and promises, but not with the relief we demand.

The Sin of Self-Protection

Not everyone is involved in flagrant sin. Many people live honorable and decent lives. But everyone develops a style of relating designed to avoid the experience of deep personal pain—and that is the sin of self-protection.

Nothing is wrong, of course, with a desire to be both physically and personally comfortable. Anything else is evidence of masochism, not maturity. No one should be criticized for exercising reasonable precaution against pain. It makes good sense to stay out of deserted streets late at night and to run out of the house when your drunken husband grabs a baseball bat and starts swinging. I also would recommend that a woman say no to an offer of marriage from a man who is mean. Protecting oneself from anticipated harm can, of course, be the proper thing to do.

The sin of self-protection to which I refer occurs when our legitimate thirst for receiving love creates a demand not to be hurt that overrides a commitment to lovingly involve ourselves with others. When that demand for self-protection interferes with our willingness to move toward others with their well-being in view, then the law of love is violated.

The violation is often subtle. It feels natural to protect ourselves, just as a desire to make money is natural for someone whose family and friends are poor. He can count on no one else to pay the bills. If he can't trust someone else to take care of what deeply matters to him, then he'd better look out for himself. Self-protective relational styles are hard to identify not only because they seem so normal but also because they are easily disguised in conventional, attractive Christian clothing.

Consider the example of a pastor who is widely respected as a humble and gentle man. His relational style is marked by a consistent effort to see the best in others and by a winsome ability to reconcile competing viewpoints, a talent he uses to keep peace in church board meetings. He is never pushy, even when he has strong opinions. He prefers to sit back in his chair, reflect on the merits of all that's been said, add a few comments in favor of his position, and then ask for a vote. People describe him as wise, patient, and utterly selfless. That is his style of relating. Most people wouldn't think to look carefully at a relational style so well received by so many. Surely any thought that this man is sinfully self-protective borders on mudslinging and witch-hunting.

It seems that when people live blameless lives in terms of the first category of sin (visible transgressions of known standards) and when their way of coming across is apparently commendable (humble, gracious), we're inclined to wrongly think that sin is no longer a problem for them, except perhaps for normal temptations with such things as lust. But (regrettably) understanding the second category of sin opens up new doors to dark rooms.

I would want to ask the pastor's wife, children, and best friend if they sense he sometimes avoids conflict that should be faced. Tough questions and hard lines are necessary in certain situations. Can this man ask those questions ("Son, I want to know where you were until 2:30 this morning. Curfew is midnight") and draw those lines ("Honey, I know how much you want new drapes, but in my judgment, our finances don't allow us to buy them now")? Or does he avoid the potential for an angry or disappointed response by remaining calm, patient— and weak? If the pastor tends to be gentle when a strong man would be firm, then I would suspect not only that his attractive relational style frustrates his wife, but also that it represents a deceitfully winsome attempt to keep things pleasant, an attempt that is weak and self-protective.

Consider how this pattern might have developed. Perhaps the pastor's father had a violent temper. If so, then early in life he experienced the painfulness of those easily triggered explosions. He learned quickly that by stating his clear preference or offering a definite opinion he ran the risk of offending his easily crossed father. Nothing hurt quite like the meanness of his dad. The words his father spoke in anger so many years ago pierced deeply then and still sting today. The pain was real—and severe enough to convince him that life itself depended on getting away from it.

If keeping his ideas and wants to himself minimized the risk of Dad's explosions, then accommodating another's viewpoint could become a habitual style of relating in threatening situations. The maturity of adulthood and the influence of Christian standards enabled him to dress his self-protective accommodation in the clothing of patient humility.

Given this possible history, notice that the purpose of his relational style is to protect himself from further frustration of his longings to be respected and loved. Arguments are avoided, rejection sidestepped, and criticism blunted by his easygoing style. His immediate effect on people is one of encouraging reciprocal warmth and discouraging hard words. The proverb, "A gentle answer turns away wrath" (Proverbs 15:1), offers apparent biblical sanction for his pattern of relating.

Certainly a gentle answer can turn away wrath (the Bible says so) and is appropriate *when the intent is to move closer to an angry person.* But when the soft answer is designed *to protect the speaker from facing an anger that threatens to undo him,* then it's not love. It's self-protective sin.

Our Styles of Relating

A person's style of relating is like the proverbial snowflake—no two are exactly alike. The design reflected in all of them is the underlying motivation of either self-protection or love. Another pastor who leads his church with strong opinions and firm stands on ticklish topics may be just as weak as the gentle pastor. If his sense of adequacy requires that he prove himself a success, and if he thinks well and communicates effectively, then his protective style of relating could be precisely the opposite of the other man's, but equally wrong.

It is also true, of course, that both the first pastor's gentleness and the second pastor's forcefulness could reflect a loving maturity that gives what one has to further God's purposes. Maturity does not homogenize: the more mature we are, the more wonderfully unique our style of relating will be. However, because the commitment to self-protection is so deeply imbedded in our fallen approach to life, we must look for it in the ways we relate.

Too often in our efforts to change, we deal only with clearly sinful behavior measured by a lack of visible conformity to biblical standards. When giving up the wrong things we do and disciplining ourselves to pray and read Scripture does not yield the desired change, then we either double our commitments to avoid wrong, do right, and learn more, or we trot off to the counselor in hope of better understanding ourselves and working through buried conflict. We rarely consider the value of what is central to real change: taking a hard look at the commitment to self-protection that displays itself most clearly in our ways of relating to people. If the core business of life is to love each other as God loves us, then a priority effort to play it safe interferes with the purpose of loving.

We were designed to love and when we do, something good develops inside. We feel clean, rich, whole. Even better, we become less concerned with how we feel and more concerned with the lives of others. But when a commitment to self-protection governs what we say, how we say it, and to whom, then a nagging discomfort creeps through our soul that demands to be soothed. We then find ourselves becoming angry when people fail to care about us as they should. If we're involved in a fellowship group that emphasizes transparency, we might "share" our disappointment with the group, and perhaps issue a plea for more involvement and real love. A demanding spirit violates the love we call for, but that spirit, which others sense in the way we relate to them, often remains unaddressed.

Bitterness develops when people don't respond to our demands. Some folks get frightened by their own anger ("if others saw my anger, they'd reject me even more") and hide it beneath depression or nervousness or obsessive thoughts about harming someone. Others express their anger more directly through outright ugliness: They may become overly critical, blatantly rebellious, or just obnoxiously sullen with those who've let them down.

The results of a self-protective approach to life are severe. The effects of loving are wonderful. We were designed by a God who wants us to trust His love enough to freely love others, not to protect our longings from further injury. And yet we love so poorly. Why? The answer is as simple as it is profound. We refuse to come to God in our thirst by abandoning our commitment to self-protection. Instead, we read our Bible and burn our porn magazines. We walk past the well of God to grab a shovel and begin digging for water in our relationships.

How foolish! But worse, how *subtly* we dig our broken wells. The gentle pastor has convinced others *and himself* that his patience is the fruit of the Spirit, when it may be nothing more than ugly self-protection. To change from the inside out requires that we repent of our self-protective commitment. We must change our mind about the best way to deal with our thirsty soul. But before we can reject our self-protection, we must first understand what it is and how we exhibit it. A careful look at our style of relating is required.

Perhaps two more illustrations will help us understand what to look for as we reflect on our relational style.

Mary

When I first met Mary, she was an attractive thirty-year-old single woman visibly active in her local church and highly respected by its leadership. She worked only part time as a dental assistant (she referred to her job as tent-making) so the bulk of her time and energy could be devoted to her volunteer church-staff position as coordinator of women's ministries. The pastor had often commended her for her dedication to Christ and more than once had commented from the pulpit, "I wish we had a dozen more Marys in this church."

Mary was a model for single Christian women: noncomplaining, friendly, hard working, eager to exploit her singleness as an opportunity for service. When asked what her feelings were about marriage, she would simply respond, "I'm open to whatever God has. If that's marriage, fine. But I have no plans to sit around waiting for a man to appear. There are too many good things to do."

Had Mary's friends been surveyed, they likely would have described her as diligent, serious, on-the-go, capable. When people thought of Mary, words like soft, womanly, and loving didn't easily come to mind.

She scheduled an appointment with me to discuss recently developing feelings of depression and a loss of energy she couldn't explain. She was deeply troubled by a growing indifference to her church work that she was unable to reverse through renewed dedication and sincere prayer. In our first meeting, I experienced her as businesslike, deliberate, and a little scared. The scared part drew me the most.

When I work with people, I pay attention to their effect on me. Does their manner create in me a desire to remain distant, to keep the conversation light, or to express strong support? Do I feel like battling with everything they say or does my time with them make me feel like a wise old man bestowing profound judgment on an eager pupil? Because we're thirsty for the relationship our soul was designed to enjoy, I assume the way we relate to one another has something to do with our thirst. And because we fear the kind of pain we know relationships can bring, we protect ourselves from the possibility of pain by adopting a style of relating that keeps people safely distant.

With that in mind, I look for the way people "pull" me to relate to them: What does their manner of relating to me pull me to do as I relate back to them? The chances are strong that their relational style will pull me to do whatever suits their purpose of self-protection. Some people keep me laughing; a serious comment would seem out of place. Others might pull me to probe deeply; simple advice to be more responsible would sound shallow. *We tend to relate to one another with the hidden purpose of maintaining our comfort and avoiding whatever sort of interaction we find threatening.* When I reflect on how I feel drawn to behave when I'm with you, I'm tuning in to the effect of your self-protective relational style, your strategy for dealing with the thirst of your soul.

With Mary, I felt uninvited. A warm comment seemed inappropriate, like asking a busy cab driver about his family as he stopped in heavy traffic to let me out. I felt pressured to think hard about her problems and to figure out an intriguing hypothesis for her to consider. I felt shoved into the role of a clever consultant rather than a caring counselor.

Although Mary was not masculine in either appearance or mannerism, I had difficulty picturing her as someone's wife. She seemed efficient at the expense of womanliness. I sensed she'd be far more comfortable discussing ministry plans at a church staff meeting than walking hand-in-hand with a man on a quiet beach. It's not wrong to feel at home in a business meeting. But when people feel out of place in close relationships, red flags appear.

As we chatted, it became clear that Mary's crisp friendliness had a purpose. When I observed that she seemed frightened by her own depression, she did not relax in my concern by simply saying, "Yes, that's true. I am afraid." Rather, she acknowledged the accuracy of my statement, and efficiently moved on to consider explanations and solutions. "Yes, I do experience some fear. I think perhaps I'm used to feeling competent in all I do, but now I've been asked to take on some jobs I may not be well suited for. I'd like your feedback about whether I'm biting off more than I can chew."

She "pulled" me to study her hypothesis and offer a professional opinion while pushing me away from compassionately exploring the fears she felt in her womanly soul. I began to wonder what prompted her to retreat from all but ministry relationships. What made her feel so threatened as a woman that she would isolate the soft, gentle and receptive parts of her soul behind her thick wall of competence and dedication?

I want to say clearly that nothing is wrong with competence or dedication. In themselves, both are commendable. *The problem lies in the function they serve.* I suspected Mary was using her natural abilities and spiritual concern to protect herself from the possibilities of pain in a close relationship. If that was correct, then she was living on the periphery of the Christian life, committed to duty, service, study, working alliances, and sociability, but not to relationships. She was neither enjoying the imperfect but real love of others nor (and more important) giving herself in love to others. Her steady top priority was her own protection against the pain of disappointing relationships.

Up to that point, no one in her life had ever questioned the function of her relational style. No one noticed she never interacted socially with a man for more than a few minutes without shifting the conversation to church matters. When a man expressed even a hint of romantic interest, she stiffened into an even more dedicated servant. No one had looked carefully at her approach to relationships. No one had loved her with wisdom.

A church filled with people like Mary (I suspect many are) is not a healthy church. Paul wrote that the body of Christ grows when each member does its work (Ephesians 4:16). The thought in that passage is that each Christian can give who he is as a redeemed, gifted person to the body of fellow believers. He has been set free from self-concern to pour himself into others. But Mary was not free. Though diligent and seemingly tireless, she was not doing the real work she was called to do. Her work in the church, though God had used it to further His purposes, was neither the expression of a heart deeply touched by God nor an effort directed above all else toward the blessing of others. Her heart was scared and her motives were self-protective. The richest parts of her being, those parts that could powerfully impact others and warmly receive the affection of others, including a man, were safely tucked away beneath a style of relating that invited people to deal with her at a ministry level and no other.

As Mary and I continued to chat, I suggested to her that she came across as more efficient than warm. She efficiently disposed of my comment by agreeing that she was a hard worker and that some might get that impression. I pressed a bit by asking how my observation made her feel. She became mildly annoyed and uncomfortable.

Several sessions went by before she admitted she did feel a bit lonely. During the months that followed she cautiously explored the disappointment she felt in key relationships. Nothing traumatic had occurred—no molesting by a cousin or beatings from an alcoholic father—but she had never felt cherished by anyone. Her father had died just a few years earlier. He had been a good man, a strong Christian who prized dedication to the Lord above all else. She could not recall a single conversation in which he warmly invited her to talk about things that deeply mattered to her. She never felt free to mention her secret crush on the new boy in school. The very thought of talking about things "like that" with her dad was strange and foreign. It simply wasn't done nor even considered.

When I asked her to imagine a very different kind of father, one who would warmly and respectfully listen to whatever she might want to share, her eyes filled with moisture. Her heart was thirsty for what she'd never had. The message from her father was clear: "You may not relax in my love. You must, instead, become more dedicated to God." She learned to deny the thirst for what she couldn't have by scolding herself for being silly and immature whenever she felt a desire to be held. And she dedicated herself all the more strongly to Christian work.

Why? Given the realities of her world, life worked better that way. She ran less risk of feeling more disappointment if she denied how badly she longed for what was in such apparently short supply. Working hard for the church won appreciation, sometimes a great deal. And that felt good. It also could give very clear signals (especially to men) that she was not in the market for a close relationship. Adding a thick veneer of spirituality completed the protective coating. Not many people are drawn to pursue a deeply personal relationship with someone who has married the church. Admiration from a distance seems more called for than direct involvement. Mary pulled people to respect and appreciate her, but never to penetrate into the secret places of her being where she longed to be loved.

As she allowed herself to feel how deeply she longed for someone to move toward her in ways her father never did, Mary began to see the self-protective purpose of her relational style. Remember an important principle: *When people deny their thirst, they cannot recognize the function of their relational style.* But when thirst is acknowledged and self-protection is unmasked, then trust in Christ can become more profound and repentance more complete. We can trust Him more when we know how badly we need what only He can provide. And the more completely our sin is exposed, the more thoroughly we can deal with it. The surgeon who sees all of the problem will do a better job than one who has spotted only part of it.

Mary today feels the impact of a disappointing world more keenly, but she is learning to relate with the courage love requires. Her relationship with the Lord is far richer than ever before. In the midst of continued busyness, she senses a quietness that allows her to say no to responsibilities she felt driven to assume before. And she now enjoys the caring involvement of friends and is warmly open to men in a way that makes her feel alive as a woman. Mary is changing from the inside out. Progress is slow (real progress usually is), but the change is real.

Frank

Consider a second illustration of self-protective relating. Frank is a successful businessman. People would describe him as full of life, talented, confident, and personable. In recent years he's become a Christian, and with characteristic zeal has quickly earned a reputation as a knowledgeable and effective Bible teacher.

Frank has it all: lovely wife, three smart kids, beautiful home, and respected place in both the business and church community. He feels really good about life and shares with passion the joys of living for Jesus.

His wife asked to see me for a few minutes after I spoke in their church. She was concerned about Ronny, their twelve-year-old son. The two older girls were doing well, but Ronny had been withdrawing from the family for several months now. She had watched him change from an unusually pleasant and mature pre-teen into a quiet, almost surly boy. She decided to speak with someone after something trivial had triggered a violent outburst of anger in which Ronny used bad language and threw a book across the room.

I asked her what her husband's thoughts about the problem were.

"I'm not sure if he's noticed the change in Ronny," she replied.

"Have you told him of your concerns?"

"Well, no, I haven't discussed it with him yet."

"Why?"

"Frank doesn't handle things like this very well. He's a wonderful father—he and Ronny play a lot of racquetball and Frank would never miss one of Ronny's basketball games. But I don't think Frank would be able to really talk with Ronny about this sort of thing."

She paused, then added with a laugh, "Frank is always so upbeat he'd probably kid around with Ronny until they were both wrestling on the floor. Then he'd figure things were okay again."

What is Frank's pull on his wife? Notice she expressed admiration for his good points but has a hard time looking squarely at his deficiencies. And she did not inform him of a problem, fearing he wouldn't deal with it effectively.

I asked her how she thought Frank might respond to her if she let him know her worries.

"Oh, I know exactly what he'd do. He'd put his arms around me, smile, and tell me I was a typical mother who worried too much. If I pressed it, he'd probably take my hand and pray with me. And that would end the discussion. I don't know what he'd do if we ever had a really big problem. One time a schoolteacher came to our home to tell us she thought our oldest daughter might be anorexic. Frank handled that by insisting she eat. It worked. But he never talked with her—and I know she was going through some pretty rough things, including some anger at her dad."

Again, hear the pull: "Things are to go well. I will be warm, spiritual, and firm, and that should keep my life running along smoothly. If there are problems beneath the surface, I don't want to hear about them. Just keep things moving along nicely."

At work Frank relishes the opportunity to make tough decisions. Bad news pumps him into even more aggressive action. He never ponders a concern longer than it takes to figure out what he must do. His record indicates an uncanny knack for knowing what course of action will keep the company moving ahead.

In church, the same thing: the building committee, the finance committee, and the stewardship committee each turn to Frank when thorny questions arise. Frank never gets discouraged and always has ideas. The Sunday school class he teaches is consistently well attended. Members corner him regularly after class to probe further into what he taught. And Frank loves it. He frequently walks into the church service late, delayed by a passionate discussion over a controversial issue he'd raised in his class.

His style of relating is clear: He's an upbeat, assertive, knowledgeable, let's-get-on-with-it kind of man. If we measure Frank by the first category of sinfulness (visible transgressions of known standards), his life is above reproach and worthy of respect. He is well qualified for leadership in the local church. He seems to manage his family well and to enjoy a good reputation.

Look more carefully at his style of relating and observe its function. The way he operates keeps him safe from ever having to admit he can't resolve a problem. He skillfully maintains a distance between himself and concerns he's not sure he can handle. He will not explore his wife's worry, he straightened out his daughter without ever inviting her to share her real burdens, and he cheerfully commits his son to God without ever facing the evidence of significant problems. Ezekiel speaks of flimsy walls that look strong because of whitewash (Ezekiel 13:10). Frank's style of relating appears to reflect maturity when in fact much of it is fueled by a commitment to self-protection.

A look inside of Frank would likely reveal a deep longing for a level of respectful involvement he's never enjoyed. Somewhere in the core of his being, Frank is desperately unsure he's adequate to face all life presents—a fear lodged deeply in every one of us. We think the fear of facing that painful inadequacy can be relieved only through the involvement of someone who trusts us with important work and equips us to do it well, someone who continues to believe in us even after we fail badly. But our experience with people does not encourage optimism that such a person exists. We are therefore left to our own resources. Frank discovered during his school and college years that his personality and ability could be used to shield him from areas of life in which he might fail. He'd found a way to maintain the image of a responsible man whom many would respect. His particular plan for self-protection fell into place.

Getting at the Core Problem

If we are to change from the inside out, then we must look carefully at our style of relating. The mark of maturity is love, and the essence of love is relating without self-protection.

Two more points need to be made in this chapter. First, people can become moral, thoughtful, disciplined, and dedicated without deeply depending on God. But living without self-protection requires profound trust in Christ.

Mary lived a commendable life while creating for herself a safe harbor where no storm could capsize her. Frank's engaging and productive style of relating kept him scurrying about his castle, protected by the moat of an affable stiff-arm which let no one, not even his wife, get close. For either of them to give up self-protection would expose them to a level of vulnerability that would eventually destroy them—unless God kept His word.

Second, when we look beneath the *details* of how we relate to the *purpose* of our relational style, we find something stubborn and ugly. It would be easier to give Mary and Frank specific instructions to do a few things differently than to dive into the reservoir of their self-protective energy.

"Mary, I think you should be more expressive. Talk to people more about your feelings. Be open to dating. When a man shows interest, accept his next request for a date."

"Frank, you must talk with your wife about Ronny. And take Ronny out for a long breakfast. Talk seriously with him. Leave the jokes for later."

Good advice to each, and advice they should heed. But both Mary and Frank could do what we tell them and never really change on the inside. *It is possible to correct what's wrong in how we relate without ever repenting of a commitment to self-protection.* The commitment itself must be exposed, looked at, and pondered. Expect a battle. We resist giving up our self-protective commitment with the desperate strength of a man fighting for his life. To move toward life without self-protection feels like suicide.

When Mary began giving up her self-protection, she was terrified. Today she is a warm, hurting, joyful, feminine, lonely, loving, grateful woman. Frank came for one session and never returned. His son is still moody but seems a little more friendly at the dinner table. His wife has faced her resentment of Frank's weakness, is working to forgive him, and feels lonelier than ever.

The demand to keep ourselves safe is strong. We look in all the wrong places for the relief our soul desires so badly, developing a style of relating designed to protect ourselves from the pain we fear. Although our self-protective strategies are foolish (even when we get the safety we want, we realize it's not what we want), we still cling to our "right" to protect ourselves. We demand that our pain be relieved. That core demand must be faced before we'll give it up through repentance and learn to re-direct our energy into love. The problem of demandingness is the topic of our next chapter.

CHAPTER EIGHT

THE PROBLEM OF DEMANDINGNESS

Change from the inside out requires that we take a disturbing look at the ugly parts of our soul. In the minds of many, that look means nothing more than confessing a tendency toward impatience or a sometimes critical spirit. Most Christians rather easily acknowledge there's more to their sinfulness than specific behaviors that violate clear standards. Of course we battle with "deeper" issues, selfish motives, and the like. But the matter is sometimes left there, at a level of non-convicting generality.

Others resist a look at inside ugliness, preferring to think more about *struggles* than *sinfulness*. "I don't have enough self-confidence. I'm just so insecure." "Why am I such a perfectionist? I worry too much, and it's driving me crazy." Problems like these generate sympathetic concern from others and an almost heroic self-pity in oneself. The exposure of sinfulness, on the other hand, provokes conviction. Strugglers feel noble, but sinners feel dirty.

In far too many churches, a sincere concern to heal the damage in people's lives has led to an understanding of people that quietly eases sin off to the side. The truth that hurting people need encouragement[1] has sometimes focused our attention on people's struggles in a way that weakens our understanding of people's sinfulness. The inevitable swing of the pendulum away from a "help the hurting" emphasis can be seen in the efforts of some conservative Christians to put the spotlight back on sin. Properly upset with the modern tendency to tone down the horror of sin by explaining it away as psychologically caused, these folks often expose sin in its most obvious forms (adultery, laziness, blame-shifting, lying, and so on) to make their point that although people may struggle, they are also sinful.

The point is well taken. Certainly we struggle as victims of other people's unkindness. We have been sinned against. But we cannot excuse our sinful responses to others on grounds of their mistreatment of us. We are responsible for what we do. We are both strugglers and sinners, victims and agents, people who hurt and people who harm.

But notice what has happened. When we look inside, we tend to think of ourselves as strugglers with buried pain and psycho-logical complexes. But when we decide it's time to get serious about our responsibility to pursue God, we come back to the surface and work at doing all we should. Struggles have come to be associated with an inside look ("let's see where you're really hurting"), and sin-fulness typically is dealt with by rearranging the outside ("it's time we stop all this introspection and get down to business. How much time are you spending with your wife?").

Sincere Christians who want to change are given two options: Find help as you honestly explore the *pain in your heart*, or assume responsibility for straightening out the *sin in your behavior*. Pain in the heart and sin in behavior: two categories we need to deal with. And yet neither guides us into the deep parts of our soul that are ugly, deformed, and diseased. Neither one helps us penetrate into the *sin in our heart* that must be addressed if we are to change from the inside out. Sin involves far more than its outward expres-sion (sin in behavior), and we struggle against worse problems than deeply imbedded psychological hang-ups (pain in the heart).

In this chapter, I want to explore neither our outside sinfulness nor our inside struggles. I want to expose the sin in our heart. I want to be more precise, however, than those who think of inter-nal sinfulness as a tendency toward impatience or an occasional critical spirit. The problem in our heart is far worse than many suspect. When we look inside, we'll bump into more than bad memories and painful feelings. An honest look will in every case eventually expose something terribly ugly—something I want to label *demandingness*.

We are a demanding people. Because we stubbornly walk right past God's water supply to dig our own wells, we end up depending for our own survival on finding water when we dig. Our efforts at self-protection *must* work. When we take the responsibility for dealing with our thirst, then survival depends on success in our digging expeditions.

We *demand* that spouses respond to our needs; we *demand* that our children exhibit the fruit of our godly training; we *demand* that our churches be sensitive to our concerns by providing certain ministries; we *demand* that slow drivers get out of the passing lane; we *demand* that no one hurt us again the way we were hurt before; we *demand* that legitimate pleasures, long denied, be ours to enjoy.

How absurd! Can you imagine an army where new recruits give orders or a company where errand boys set policy? And yet mere people shout orders to the universe. Such foolishness is the inevitable result of taking responsibility for securing our own happiness, a burden that's simply too heavy for our shoulders. When we assume responsibility for what we desperately require but cannot control, we irrationally demand that our efforts succeed.

Wedged tightly in our thirsty soul is the ugly disease of a demanding spirit. Change from the inside out requires that we face our problem of demandingness and do something about it. The spirit of demandingness must be identified, recognized in all its ugliness, and abandoned through repentance. Think with me about the problem from three angles: (1) how God views the problem, (2) how the problem develops, and (3) what God does with it.

How God Views the Problem

In Numbers 9:15-23, the record tells how the Israelites were led through the wilderness. They were to watch a special cloud in the sky (a cloud that became a ball of fire at night to ensure visibility), to break camp when the cloud began moving and follow it wherever it led, and to camp again when the cloud stopped. The point of the narrative isn't difficult to grasp: When the cloud moved, they moved, and when it stopped, they stopped. Two or three sentences seem quite enough to communicate how things worked. The *Reader's Digest* condensed version of the Bible shares that view. The nine verses that relate the story in the unabridged text are reduced to one verse in the condensed version. The necessary message is conveyed just as well in one verse as in nine. Or is it?

Read the full text recorded below. Notice its almost insulting repetitiveness. An editor of one of my earlier books once told me I had a love affair with adjectives. Cutting out unnecessary words, he said, could substantially shorten the book and make it more readable. No writer enjoys being told he's wordy. And in my less noble moments, I've often wondered what the same editor would say if he were given these nine verses as part of a manuscript from an unidentified author.

> On the day the tabernacle, the Tent of the Testimony, was set up, the cloud covered it from evening till morning the cloud above the tabernacle looked like fire. That is how it continued to be; the cloud covered it, and at night it looked like fire. Whenever the cloud lifted from above the Tent, the Israelites set out; wherever the cloud settled, the Israelites encamped. At the Lord's command the Israelites set out, and at his command they encamped. As long as the cloud stayed over the tabernacle, they remained in camp. When the cloud remained over the tabernacle a long time, the Israelites obeyed the Lord's order and did not set out. Sometimes the cloud was over the tabernacle only a few days; at the Lord's command they would encamp, and then at his command they would set out. Sometimes the cloud stayed only from evening till morning, and when it lifted in the morning, they set out. Whether by day or by night, whenever the cloud lifted, they set out. Whether the cloud stayed over the tabernacle for two days or a month or a year, the Israelites would remain in camp and not set

out; but when it lifted, they would set out At the LORD'S command they encamped, and at the LORD'S command they set out. They obeyed the LORD'S order, in accordance with his command through Moses.

We must conclude that either the writer of Numbers needed a better editor for his work or there is a message in the passage that fewer words could not convey. A high view of biblical inspiration presumes the latter. What, then, is the message?

Think about what actually must have happened: thousands of Israelites trudging through a tedious desert, some probably ill, others feeling energetic, still others bothered by leg cramps. I can picture one out-of-shape, middle-aged father of four puffing along, yelling at his kids to stop bickering, worried about the chest pains that get worse the more he walks. He glances up regularly to see if the cloud is showing any sign of slowing down and feels annoyed as he watches it floating on ahead.

"Whoever is blowing that cloud along," he grumbles under his breath, "sure doesn't know what I'm going through—or else He doesn't care. My wife can't handle the kids, my angina is kicking up—we need a break. I have to stop or I'm going to collapse. Please, Lord, stop the cloud." But it keeps on moving.

An hour or two passes by and, strangely, his chest pains stop. He feels a burst of energy, sort of a "runner's high." His older boy is carrying the tired toddler. He looks over at his wife and she's grinning. "Maybe God knew continued walking was the best thing for all of us." He feels a new bounce in his steps—and just then the cloud stops.

The man looks up in puzzled disgust, unable to understand what's happening. "When I'm too tired to continue, God makes me press on. When I feel like covering ground, I'm told to take a break."

With the rest of the crowd, he obediently stops, unloads the animals, and sets up camp. When he stretches out on a blanket, he begins to realize how badly he needed the rest. Fatigue sweeps through his body, and he gratefully yawns and closes his eyes.

Just as he dozes peacefully into the first stages of a deep sleep, his wife shakes him awake: "The cloud started moving. We've got to get going again."

Perhaps my story is a bit fanciful (certainly the biblical text includes no such record), but with the number of people whose pace was directed by that cloud, there must have been at least a few, perhaps many, who felt insensitively treated.

The way God arranges things sometimes seems uniquely designed to frustrate us: a tire goes flat on the way to the hospital; the sink backs up an hour before overnight company arrives; a friend lets you down during a time when you most need support; you suddenly develop laryngitis the day of your presentation to important buyers. In times of frustration, our High Priest sometimes seems more callous to our needs than sympathetic.

We pray, asking God to hear our cry, pleading with Him to let nothing else go wrong. I wonder if sometimes the passion in our prayers reflects more of a *demand* than a *petition*. Frustration is excellent soil for growing a demanding spirit. It is therefore important that we handle difficulties well, allowing them to mature us rather than to push us toward demandingness.

The beginning of a proper response to frustrating circumstances is a clear recognition of who's in charge. To handle frustration by reminding ourselves how much God loves us is a good second step, but not the first one. We must take our place as a creature before our Creator and *then* explore the wonder of our Creator's loving character. An awareness of God's love casts out our fear, but subjection to His authority deals with our demandingness.

The passage in Numbers repeats one theme again and again: When the cloud moves, you move; when the cloud stops, you stop. I wonder if God is saying something like this:

"I know My ways will seem to ignore your concerns at times. I want you to trust Me when you feel unusually tired and I call on you to get up. I want you to trust Me when you're eager to serve and I put you on hold. But you will never learn to trust Me until you come to terms with My authority. Trust will never emerge from a demanding spirit. Let's start with a clear understanding: I give the orders. You do what you're told. With that as a beginning, you will eventually taste My goodness and the richness of fellowship with Me and come to trust Me deeply."

No degree of personal discomfort, whether leg cramps on a long walk or a family falling apart after years of responsible effort, can ever justify a demanding spirit. Problems may fuel a demanding spirit but never justify it. God is unalterably opposed to a demanding attitude on the part of His creatures no matter how severe their suffering. His ears are opened wide to hear cries of lament and pleas for help, but He will not come to a negotiating table to consider terms from angry people. God opposes the proud who demand but He gives grace to the humble who express their hurt.

How the Problem Develops

Because we're fallen people who are looking for satisfaction through our own efforts, we each carry the infection of demandingness within us. Whether the infection spreads and destroys spiritual life or weakens into a low-grade fever that occasionally rises depends on a variety of factors. The record of Job's suffering provides a clear illustration of how the potential for demandingness, long dormant in his life, can develop into a crippling disease that requires direct intervention from God. A brief study of Job's life is a good backdrop for discerning the conditions in which demandingness can best develop.

As the biblical narrative begins, Job is hit with a series of devastating disappointments. First his oxen and donkeys are killed, along with the servants tending them, by vicious marauders. Before the messenger who told Job the bad news has completed his report, a second messenger rushes in to announce that lightning has just burned up Job's sheep and more servants. A third messenger interrupts the second to tell Job that another band of raiders has just stolen his camels and killed the servants who were watching them. While Job is reeling from these three reports of terrible news, a fourth person appears to bring the news that the house in which

Job's sons and daughters were enjoying a dinner party has just collapsed, burying all of his children.

Suddenly, Job was financially ruined and bereaved of his children. He responded to the disaster by falling to the ground in worship: "Naked I came from my mother's womb, and naked I will depart. The LORD gave and the LORD has taken away; may the name of the LORD be praised" (Job 1:21).

But more troubles were still ahead. In the next chapter, we learn that God specifically permitted Satan to add sorrow upon sorrow by causing Job's body to break out in painful sores, from his head to his feet. Job had been a healthy, wealthy, upright family man. Now he was a diseased, impoverished man who had just buried all ten of his children—and all this with God's definite permission. If ever a man's life did not support the gospel of health, wealth, and happiness, it was Job's.

Add to this marital tension. Job's wife had had enough. She encouraged him to curse God, perhaps in the hope that God might strike him dead. In her mind, only death seemed adequate relief for her husband.

But Job replied with unusual maturity: "Shall we accept good from God, and not trouble?" The inspired record specifically informs us, "In all this, Job did not sin in what he said" (Job 2:10). There is no hint of a demanding spirit of complaint and bitter self-pity in Job's *initial* response to tragedy.

And that is often how it works. In the immediate aftermath of difficult times, we manage to mobilize our resources and cling to God as we press on. But I wonder if the strength to deal with tough times is sometimes supported by a quiet but strong hope that a good response from us will bring a quicker end to our trials and a return to better times: "God, I've learned the lesson from these difficulties. See how maturely I'm handling them? It's okay now to make things easier for me."

It seems to be true that the longer we must wait for hoped-for relief, the greater the struggle becomes to trust God's goodness. Much of what looks like trust may reflect little more than the confident expectation of restored blessing.

Three of Job's friends came to offer comfort. For one entire week, they wisely gave him only their presence, sitting quietly in supportive silence. Job's misery was too severe for mere words to be meaningful.

After seven days of numbness, Job broke the silence by expressing the anguish of his soul. It's good to pour out before another the sadness and pain we deeply feel inside. The psalmists expressed their heartfelt lament. Our Lord experienced His anguish so deeply in the garden that blood broke through His skin. Job gave vent to his pain by stating that his life was so horrible, it would have been better had he never been born. The man was hurting profoundly. To describe his pain in terms of a longing for what he did not have borders on sterile understatement, but it's true. Job was designed for blessing (as we all are), but he experienced severe trial.

As we continue looking at Job's way of handling his problems, we need to keep in mind an important principle: *When things do not go well, especially for an extended time, when our heart is filled with more pain than joy, the temptation to let our desire for relief become a demand is strongest.* And the more severe the pain, the stronger the temptation.

Job's first friend, a man named Eliphaz, encouraged Job's latent tendency to demand by suggesting he take his case before God (Job 5:8). Job understandably wanted relief, but he had no means of attaining it. Eliphaz planted a thought in Job's mind that eventually developed into a false hope—and a demand. Eliphaz reacted to Job's sufferings by looking for an explanation he could understand. There must be a reason for the sudden tragedies that befell Job and, if that reason could be found, then perhaps it would suggest a way to reverse things and restore comfort. That reasoning, I believe, was what led Eliphaz to think Job had a case to present before God, an argument that would prevail in God's courtroom.

People desperate for relief eagerly grab onto strategies they might recognize as foolish in moments of more sober reflection.[2] Job was vulnerable to the appeal of a strategy for finding relief. "Oh, that I might have my request, that God would grant what I hope for" (Job 6:8).

Bildad, Job's second friend, continued the theme by assuring Job that if he'd plead with God from a pure heart, God would rouse Himself on his behalf and restore things to the way they should be (Job 8:5-6).

Zophar, the third friend, accused Job of harboring some evil in his life and assured him that if he'd get rid of his sin and recommit his life to God, the Lord would surely remove his shame (Job 11:11-15).

Notice that much of what the three friends said is good, but none of them was sensitive to the problem of demandingness. Each was looking for some way to improve Job's condition without taking precautions against nourishing a demanding spirit. "If you do this," they said, "then God will give you that."

Job pondered the advice, then rejected it in despair. "Though one wished to dispute with [God], he could not answer him one time out of a thousand" (Job 9:3). "I'm sorry, gentlemen," Job was saying. "It won't work. You're suggesting I challenge God. But if I were to take Him on in oral debate, I wouldn't be able to win one round out of a thousand. Even if my case were airtight, I still can't imagine disputing with God."

But Job's pain continued. Nothing is quite as unsettling as a chronic ache when there is no promise of relief. As hope fades, patient trust erodes into demandingness, indicating that what passed for trust may have been little more than a false confidence that God would eventually (within a month? a year? two years?) give us what we wanted so badly. When our prayers go unanswered for longer than we expected, our confidence is sometimes shaken. The veneer of trust may then be stripped away to expose a demanding spirit quietly growing beneath the surface.

Some years ago, I received a letter from a young woman thanking me for the help she'd received through one of my books. She told me her husband had deserted her without warning, leaving her alone to care and provide for three small children. As she read the book, she felt greatly encouraged by the idea that Christ is sufficient for everything we need.

Many months after I'd received that letter, a young woman approached me during a break in one of my seminars and told me she was the deserted wife who'd written the letter. Within the first few minutes of our conversation, I found myself feeling strangely uncomfortable with her confident glow as she talked about the joy of trusting the Lord.

I reacted to my discomfort by asking, "You have felt very encouraged by the truth that Christ is enough. But help me understand exactly what you mean. What is Christ enough for?"

"Oh, for everything I need," she quickly responded with a smile.

"What do you need? What are you expecting the Lord to do?"

"Bring my husband back, of course. My three little girls need a daddy. And I need a husband. I just know God will work in his heart to bring him back. I don't know when, but I know it will happen."

When I indicated I knew of no biblical basis for her confidence, her mood abruptly changed. "How can you even doubt it? Do you think it's been easy for me to be alone? If God is as faithful as He says He is, then He'll bring my husband back. He must!"

As she finished speaking, her voice was filled with desperate anger, the anger of a demanding spirit. She was a deeply hurting woman (pain in the heart), and she was now visibly bitter (sin in behavior), but the core problem that needed attention was a demanding spirit (sin in the heart). Her "trust" in God was rooted not in unconditional confidence in His character and sovereign plan but rather in a hope that He'd relieve her suffering in the way she desired.[3] The longer fulfillment was postponed, the more demanding she became as she "waited upon God."

Unrelenting pain is a most suitable environment in which to grow a demanding spirit. Notice what happened to Job as his sorrow continued unabated.

"I loathe my very life; therefore I will give free rein to my complaint and speak out in the bitterness of my soul. I will say to God: Do not condemn me, but tell me what charges you have against me" (Job 10:1-2).

The longer he remained in misery, the more unfair his situation seemed. When his soul was weighed down with unbearable suffering and there was no relief in sight, his demanding spirit finally came into full bloom: "I desire to speak to the Almighty and to argue my case with God" (Job 13:3). Quite a shift for a man who earlier had dismissed the prospect of debating with God as futile. He now seems convinced that he really *has a case*!

That belief is typical of a demanding spirit. To insist on something, we must first persuade ourself that what we're after is deserved and legitimate, that we have a solid basis for our demands. And nothing persuades us more completely that our weary soul deserves a break than continued heartache. After years of enduring a thoughtless, non-communicative husband, a wife may come to believe that demanding a better companion is entirely justified. The line between legitimate desiring and illegitimate demanding is thin and easily crossed.

Job had become convinced he had a case. No longer did he pray for relief; he was ready to demand it. The intensity of his conviction is reflected in his well-known statement, "Though he slay me, yet will I hope in him." This verse is often held up as an example of fervent faith, but notice the second half of the verse: "I will surely defend my ways to his face" (Job 13:15). He goes on to say, "Now that I have prepared my case, I know I will be vindicated. Can anyone bring charges against me? If so, I will be silent and die" (Job 13:18-19).

Far from humbly yielding to the decisions of a sovereign God, Job strongly asserts that he deserves better treatment than he has received. If God takes his life, Job pledges to go to his grave convinced that if the facts were known, it would be clear to everyone that he has been mistreated.

Each of us has been a victim of someone else's sinfulness. We've been mistreated. It's unfair. But when the hurt caused by others drives us not to trust in God and return love for evil, but rather to demand relief, then God's failure to cooperate with our demand makes Him seem less like a concerned friend and more like a cruel enemy. Listen to Job's perception of God:

"Surely, O God, you have worn me out; you have devastated my entire household. You have bound me—and it has become a witness; my gauntness rises up and testifies against me. God assails me and tears me in his anger and gnashes his teeth at me; my opponent fastens on me his piercing eyes" (Job 16:7-9).

So many Christians report they have trouble believing God really loves them. Others speak glowingly of Christ's wonderful love, but with more emphasis in their voice than burning in their soul. Why does God seem uncaring and so far removed from the struggles we endure?

Perhaps part of the problem is that we have definite plans for achieving happiness, or at least for finding relief. Those plans are rooted in ways of thinking about life that are so inherently imbedded in our makeup that we never think to question them. We tend to measure someone's love by their degree of cooperation with our plans. God's refusal to help us pursue our goals (and His insistence that we yield our plans to His) makes Him seem unconcerned about our happiness. The heavens turn into a ceiling, above which our prayers never rise. Our mind invents an image of a God who sits unmoved by our pain and annoyed by our complaining. Our fervent pleas for Him to do what our view of rightness and compassion would require go unheeded.

Job's conviction that the weight of morality was on his side grew stronger. He seemed to imagine that arguments on his behalf would persuade anyone, including God, that urgent corrective measures were in order. But God remained impassive, coldly unimpressed with Job's demands.

Eventually Job exclaimed, "Though I cry, 'I've been wronged!' I get no response; though I call for help, there is no justice" (Job 19:7).

When difficult problems grow worse, it's tempting to give up on God. When the ultimate Source of power refuses to take up our just cause, then whatever is required to find relief seems entirely warranted. How can you blame a starving man, especially one who is starving through no fault of his own, for stealing an apple? Unremitting struggle tends to blur our lines of moral distinctions. Things that are clearly wrong become less offensive to our conscience when they provide our only hope for relief.

Again, notice the central problem: It is neither the hurt in our soul (it's okay to hurt) nor our desire for relief and satisfaction (it's okay to thirst); it is the *demand*. When we demand relief of our thirst now, we're in danger of slipping from a biblical ethic into a morality of pragmatism: whatever eases our pain is justified. The result is often blatant moral compromise and a ruined life. Others who both hurt and demand may not turn their backs on God by living in obvious sin, but they continue to deal with Him from the premise that their demands have merit.

People who hurt hate to lose hope. But the means of sustaining hope may be to reason that someday (before heaven) God will make life easier. Somehow He'll arrange things so we can have what "we know" is essential to our happiness. Perhaps our husband will leave us for another woman, freeing us to "biblically" marry the man we have quietly loved for years. Maybe God will touch our teenage daughter at youth camp; God knows our prayers rise out of a heart shredded by her defiant sullenness. We simply can't take much more.

When we still "look to God" for the required relief, the task becomes to discover how God can be persuaded of the reasonableness of our petition. If only we could convince Him that a good Father should give His suffering children a break. When the Israelites cried out in their affliction in Egypt, God heard and delivered them. Why won't He respond to our suffering? There must be a way to get Him to see things from our point of view.[4]

Listen to Job as he expresses his desire to meet God and to make his point in God's presence:

> Then Job replied: "Even today my complaint is bitter; his hand is heavy in spite of my groaning. If only I knew where to find him; if only I could go to his dwelling! I would state my case before him and fill my mouth with arguments. I would find out what he would answer me, and consider what he would say. Would he oppose me with great power? No, he would not press charges against me. There an upright man could present his case before him, and I would be delivered forever from my judge." (Job 23:1-7)

Most of us have in some form gone through the same imaginative exercise: If only we could have an audience with God! Think of the opportunities a British citizen might enjoy if he could speak directly to the Queen! But still there is a resigned awareness that even a personal visit with God might not bring the hoped-for results. Job wearily admitted that God is too independent to be controlled by his petition:

> But he stands alone, and who can oppose him? He does whatever he pleases. He carries out his decree against me, and many such plans he still has in store. That is why I am terrified before him; when I think of all this, I fear him. (Job 23:13-15)

Job's admission is in his favor. The person who concedes that God may not do for him what seems so right is farther along in his understanding of God than one who cheerfully expects God to make everything better. The naive optimist prefers romantic fiction to real-life biography. He must. The facts of experience would shatter his cheeriness. The faith of a happy optimist is like sweet icing on a cake: it is sweet and decorative but utterly lacking in the nourishment needed for health.

Job was no frothy optimist—far from it. That much was good. But his realistic admission that God may not accede to his requests led not to humble faith in a God who does all things after the counsel of His perfect will, but to a demandingness that created angry despair: "God may not come through, and He probably won't, but *He should!*"

We are so deeply committed to our own well-being that anyone who blocks our path to the joy we desire becomes the object of our wrath while we suffer with noble grief. "How can He treat me like that? It's just so wrong. Well, I'll just press on even though I hurt."

That attitude is utterly abhorrent to God. It's ugly. Our Lord instructed us to love others as we love ourself, to be as concerned with someone else's well being as we already are with our own. The command is staggering. The more I understand what love requires, the more I realize how poorly I love, and the more awed I become by Christ's love. God really expects me to focus on my response to others, measuring it by the lofty standards of divine love, even when the one I'm trying to love is failing me badly.

But that is completely alien to our natural way of operating. A response like that violates every normal sensibility of our darkened mind. It simply doesn't seem right that we should be so badly disappointed. We tend to get stuck on the painful fact of our disappointment. To live without regard for continued disappointment seems as unnatural as using our ears to eat and our mouths to hear.

We may demand that something go our way, that our daughter smile and say, "Sure, Dad, I'd love to have lunch with you. Thanks for asking." Such a demand seems eminently reasonable and healthy, even noble. And that's one of the terrible stings about a demanding spirit: It feels good. A disease without symptoms is bad enough, but a disease that increases our feelings of well-being while it slowly destroys our health is worse.

Demandingness is a serious problem partly because it rarely feels like a problem. We may actually feel stronger and more alive when we pursue our demands and rehearse to ourself their credibility. It's possible to sense a flush of counterfeit spirituality as we approach God in a vigorous attitude of petition that's fueled by a demanding spirit. "Dear Lord, You know how much I'm hurting because of our family tensions. I come to You now in faith, believing You will answer my prayers to restore our family's joys. Lead me, dear Lord, as I seek to take hold of my responsibilities as a husband and father." The prayer may be a worthy one and its effect may be calmness and strength as the man seeks to love his family properly. Or it may reflect an underlying demand that God restore his family's unity, a demand that gives the man confidence as he moves toward his family. If more family tensions arise, the man's good feelings may become self-righteous resentment toward the One who allowed the additional problem.

Christian growth requires that we surface the tendency to demand. It must be identified, exposed in all its ugliness, and abandoned. Otherwise, deep change will not occur.

What God Does with a Demanding Spirit

The last few chapters of the book of Job provide one of the most dramatic accounts in Scripture of God intervening directly in someone's life. A remarkable conversation is recorded in which God dealt with a demanding spirit.

In the midst of terrible calamities, events that God specifically allowed to take place, Job had developed a demanding spirit. He eventually became so persuaded of the rightness of his demands that he passionately desired an opportunity to state his case directly to God. God granted his wish, but the encounter did not proceed as Job had anticipated. Listen again to what Job thought would happen if God agreed to meet with him:

> I would state my case before him and fill my mouth with arguments. I would find out what he would answer me, and consider what he would say. Would he oppose me with great power? No, he would not press charges against me. There an upright man could present his case before him, and I would be delivered forever from my judge.
> (Job 23:4-7)

Job apparently expected God would listen to what he had to say, pull slowly on His beard, and reply, "Job, thanks for sharing your perspective on things. You've got a point. Frankly, I really hadn't seen things quite the way you see them. Look, I've made a bit of an error but I'll straighten it all out right away."

Put this boldly, its absurdity is obvious. But a demanding spirit disguises its ridiculous thinking in the clothing of fervent petition. In chapter 38, we get a rare opportunity to see God respond directly to Job's demands and to learn how He likely responds to ours.

God gave Job the audience he'd wanted so badly. But things didn't go as expected. From the very first moment God appeared, Job must have realized he was in for a difficult time: "The LORD answered Job out of the storm" (Job 38:1). No gentle voice to soothe Job's anguish, no warm invitation to still his troubled heart by thinking about the mansions under construction in a better world.

When a suffering saint pours out the sorrow of his soul, our Lord reveals Himself as his Great High Priest, a caring Advocate who is touched by his struggles. But when that sorrow has been twisted into a bitter spirit of demandingness, his lament is met by the steely glare of a Surgeon, ready to cut out the disease with a glistening scalpel. God thunders out a challenge: "Brace yourself like a man; I will question you, and you shall answer me" (Job 38:3).

Let me digress for a moment to underscore the point of God's words. When I was a student in college, I took several courses from a brilliant philosophy professor who was a confirmed atheist. After my first course, I appointed myself the representative of Christianity to this man, thinking I might reach him with the gospel as I stood clearly for the truth of God's Word.

In retrospect, it's not difficult to see that my approach was neither wise nor winsome. During further course work with this instructor, I sat in the back row of his classroom, listening eagerly for a flaw in his logic. When I thought I found one, I quickly raised my hand to question his argument. At the time, I assumed he admired my inquiring mind and flattered myself that he was quite intrigued with my cogent reasoning. Now, as a professor myself who occasionally must endure similar students, I think I better understand what he undoubtedly felt.

By the time the semester was drawing to a close, I had tried my teacher's patience with a liberal assortment of incisive observations. He'd finally had enough. When I raised my hand one more time, he abruptly stood up, looked at me with a withering fierceness, and spoke with measured intensity: "Crabb, get your chair and come up on the platform with me. We will spend the remainder of the class period, and all afternoon if necessary, considering your objections to my positions. It's time we have it out."

My professor happened to be a philosopher of some renown, impressive not only to college juniors who were pondering Kant and Hegel for the first time, but also to colleagues at prestigious institutions who respected his critique of various systems of thought.

I had never intended to actually debate the man; I'd merely wanted to share a few thoughts for him to consider. Or so I'd thought when I'd shared them. He had properly recognized my jabs as an effort to undermine his entire system of thought and to replace it with mine.

When he summoned me to the platform with the cool authority of a judge, I felt terror-stricken. I knew I was out of my league. If I felt scared out of my wits when a brilliant unbelieving scholar challenged me to a debate about his area of expertise, imagine how Job must have felt when the omnipotent sovereign Lord of creation called upon him to support his position that the universe was being poorly run.

Perhaps the first step in learning humility is to consider who it is we think must change. A demand that things be different represents an accusation against God, a charge that He's guilty of mismanagement and negligence in His duties.

God began to put things in perspective for Job by requiring him to establish his credentials for debating with the Creator, to pass a "bar exam" proving his competence to present a case.

First question: Job, "where were you when I laid the earth's foundation? Tell me, if you understand. Who marked off its dimensions? Surely you know!" (Job 38:4-5).

"Uh, I'm not sure I do. Can I think on that one and come back to it later?"

God continued: "Have you ever given orders to the morning, or shown the dawn its place?" (Job 38:12). In other words, "Job, do you tell the sun when it's time to rise, or do you merely set your alarm clock to wake you when it does? Are you the creator and sustainer and sovereign of the universe, or are you a mere mortal?"

Next question: "What is the way to the abode of light? And where does darkness reside? ... Surely you know, for you were already born! You have lived so many years!" (Job 38:19,21).

Sarcastic words, piercing—like a sharp blade that cuts deep, guided by the steady hand of a Master Surgeon.

The first examination came to an end when God issued the challenge, "Will the one who contends with the Almighty correct him? Let him who accuses God answer him!" (Job 40:2).

The questions had been asked. The point had been made. The demanding person who had earlier expected to fill his mouth with arguments had been humbled. Job's words indicate real movement toward humility, just as half-completed surgery represents good progress toward health. Movement, but not enough. Progress, but not cure. Listen to a changing man: "I am unworthy—how can I reply to you? I put my hand over my mouth. I spoke once, but I have no answer—twice, but I will say no more" (Job 40:4-5).

Job was changing from the inside out. His demanding spirit had been weakened. Now it was time for the deathblow.

When God goes to work on a human soul, He never settles for a half-cure. "I got most of the cancer" is not a comforting report from your surgeon. God invades the deepest recesses of our deceitful heart to ruthlessly expose what needs to be changed. His *acceptance* of us on the basis of Calvary and His *understanding* of our hurt provide the context for His work in our heart, but relentless *exposure* of our arrogant demandingness begins the healing. As we learn to recognize, hate, and abandon our demanding spirit and to entrust the Lord with our deepest longings, we clean the inside of the cup and dish.

God continued to expose Job's demandingness through a second exam. While the first dealt more with a comparison between God's power and Job's weakness, the second began by shifting the focus to the issue of morality.

"Brace yourself like a man," God said. In other words, "I'm not done with you yet. You're not dismissed. You have utterly failed My first exam. You could not answer even one question. Now, let's see how you do on a second test."

God then underscored the point He wanted to make by asking, "Would you discredit my justice? Would you condemn me to justify yourself?" (Job 40:8).

The issue the question raised is this: Who is in a position to legislate what is right and wrong? Suffering can be intense, but no level of suffering justifies us in deciding how we *should* be treated. Nor can pain be so severe that sinful strategies for finding relief become acceptable. No matter how much relief of intolerable pain self-protection might provide, we can never violate love without sinning.

God ended the second exam with a strange sentence: "[God] is king over all that are proud" (Job 41:34). Proud people demand. They assume they have that right. But God set the record straight: there is no one whose high estimate of himself qualifies him to tell God what to do. And that final point emphasizes a central principle of living in God's world: the necessary foundation for any relationship with God is a recognition that God is God and we are not. We therefore have no business demanding anything of anyone, no matter how fervently our soul longs for relief from pain. It is wrong to internally demand that your loved one become a Christian or your spouse stop drinking or your biopsy be negative or your rebellious child straighten up. Desire much, pray for much, but demand nothing. To trust God means to demand nothing.

Job got the message. The Surgeon had once again done His work well. Listen to the words of a man whose heart had been changed, words that reflect change from the inside out.

"Surely I spoke of things I did not understand, things too wonderful for me to know ... My ears had heard of you but now my eyes have seen you. Therefore I despise myself and repent in dust and ashes" (Job 42:3,5-6).

Recall how Job spoke before the change:

"I will ... speak out" (Job 10:1).

"I will say to God: Do not condemn me" (Job 10:2).

"I desire to speak to the Almighty and to argue my case with God" (Job 13:3).

"I will surely defend my ways to his face" (Job 13:15).

"Though I cry ... I get no response; though I call for help, there is no justice" (Job 19:7).

"I would state my case before him and fill my mouth with arguments" (Job 23:4).

"I sign now my defense ... let my accuser put his indictment in writing" (Job 31:35).

When God dealt with Job's demanding spirit by exposing its ugliness, Job realized that for a man to demand anything of God is sheer madness; it is grotesque. The beginning of maturity is an estimate of oneself that makes demandingness unthinkable. And that estimate develops when we confront the reality of who God is and who we are.

A noted saint was asked shortly before his death how he handled the fact that God was allowing him to die despite the prayers of thousands for his healing. His answer was this: "When I am in the presence of God, it seems uniquely unbecoming to demand anything."

"The fear of the LORD is the beginning of wisdom" (Psalm 111:10). To stand in awe of God even when things are hard is as important as it is difficult. When we measure ourself against God, we begin to understand the absurdity and arrogance of demanding anything, including the relief of pain we fervently desire. It's one thing to petition with urgency and passion, to weep in anguish, and to plead for relief. It's quite another to demand that the will of the Almighty be one with our own.

We are told that Job repented. Of what? Job abandoned his demand for relief, realizing it is uniquely unbecoming to demand anything of God.

How does one repent of a demanding spirit? What does it mean to trust God with our thirst and to abandon our self-protection? Before we consider these questions in Part Four, perhaps further discussion of what it takes to expose the dirt inside the cup and dish is in order.

NOTES

1. I have devoted an entire book to thinking through this concern—*Encouragement: The Key to Caring*, Crabb and Allender (Grand Rapids: Zondervan, 1984).

2. People sometimes bargain with God: "I promise to never be immoral again if You cure my disease" or "I'll get more involved in church if that pay raise comes through." I wonder how much spiritual fervor is really an effort to manipulate God—not to put ourself in line for blessing, but to demand it.

3. Nothing is wrong with confidence that God will deeply satisfy the desires of a heart that delights in Him. That confidence has biblical sanction. But delighting in God involves an utter surrender to His care, a surrender that cannot co-exist with a demanding spirit.

4. An interesting verse in Hosea (7:14) indicates that God responds when people cry out from their hearts but not when they wail upon their beds. Part Four of this book will more thoroughly discuss the difference between crying over our problems and repenting of our demandingness. God does not normally respond to the former, but He always hears a repentant follower.

CHAPTER NINE

EXPOSING WRONG DIRECTIONS

Doing good things does not automatically turn us into good people. Spending hours in Bible study, witnessing regularly, avoiding worldly amusements, and generously giving time and money to the Lord's work are godly things to do, but they are not sufficient in themselves to produce deep change.

Most of us know people who commendably model each of these virtues but who relate deeply to no one. Apparently, the practice of these and similar disciplines does not guarantee a life that draws people to Christ by the sheer power of its attractive depth. In order to be changed into a person whose life has that power, we must deal with the *inside* of the cup and dish. We must expose the sinfulness in our deceitful heart and then learn how to clean it up.

Exposure is no easy matter. The deceitful character of our heart helps us believe that things are quite a bit better than they really are. No matter how sincerely we want to identify the wrongs in our life, we still have a hard time seeing the subtle way a demanding spirit infects our style of relating.

Obvious concerns (skipping church, getting drunk, cheating on our mates, attending questionable movies) are much easier to deal with and therefore tend to receive priority attention in our efforts to become holy. We can spot them more easily, determine their sinfulness more clearly (just ask your pastor), and change them more explicitly. We know whether we walked into a movie theater or not. But have we sacrificed someone's feelings in order to build our own self-image? Have we compromised an opportunity to love in order to stay safe? Those kinds of offenses are much more difficult to recognize, and even when we recognize them, we don't always call them sin. We're inclined to say, "Well, that's my personality" or "I guess that's just the way I am" or "Why be so picky? That kind of self-analysis would make me question everything I do."

Not only do our self-protective patterns appear innocent, sometimes they look absolutely noble. Our relational style may appear humble, strong, thoughtful, bold, friendly; the sinful, demanding spirit that fuels it may remain disguised. Leaders protect themselves from failure by working hard—and are admired for their zeal. Husbands avoid conflict with their wives by extra acts of kindness—and expect appreciation. Church members strive for popularity by becoming unusually friendly with the social leaders in the fellowship—and are regarded as hospitable.

A determination to maintain personal safety, no matter how attractively disguised, is always ugly. To demand anything, including what we believe is essential to our well-being, reflects arrogant pride, a sin that tops the list of what God detests. Yet sin in the heart so often goes unnoticed. Very few people seem concerned with the possibility that their approach to relationships may be seriously deficient. We simply do not see, nor do we care to, that the way we "come across" to others may grow out of a demanding commitment to self-preservation lodged stubbornly in our heart. Though our Lord taught that trying to save our life will always fail, we rarely consider how we may be working to save our life in the way we relate to people.

In speaking to the Pharisees, Christ ruthlessly exposed the sinfulness clothed in their fine speech when He said, "How can you who are evil say anything good? For out of the overflow of the heart the mouth speaks … But I tell you that men will have to give account on the day of judgment for every careless word they have spoken. For by your words you will be acquitted, and by your words you will be condemned" (Matthew 12:34,36-37).

The point is clear: If we are to make our words good, we must first clean up their source. If we are to love genuinely, we must first pull up the evil root of self-protection in our sinful heart: "Above all else, guard your heart, for it is the wellspring of life" (Proverbs 4:23). For thirsty people bent on digging our own wells, guarding the heart must include developing a sensitivity to the ways in which we demand of others what we think we need for our satisfaction. Without recognizing our self-protective style of relating and repenting of it, how can we say anything good? How can we love?

Seeing Ourself Clearly

We must learn to evaluate the things we do and say as we interact with people to see where the disease of demandingness has spread. And we must proceed with the evaluation process without becoming hopelessly consumed with morbid introspection. If self-understanding is the ultimate goal of an inside look, then we will likely fall into the quicksand of introspection. Coming up with clever theories about ourself, why we feel this way and why we do that, is not in itself a profitable exercise. *The sole value of an inside look is measured by its helpfulness in moving us toward greater love, both for God and for others.*

Sometimes the disease we're looking for is obvious, at least to an observer. I once counseled with a husband who, within the first few minutes of our appointment, made clear his reason for coming. He enjoyed oral sex; his wife, whom he had insisted come with him and who sat looking both timid and angry, was disgusted by it. With the authority of a judge, he informed me that she was violating God's command to regard her body as belonging to her husband (1 Corinthians 7:4). He then requested ("ordered" might better describe it) that I deal with his wife about her nonsubmissive sinfulness. When I suggested he might be violating the law of love by demanding the gratification he desired, he dismissed the novel idea and impatiently waited for me to challenge his wife.

The issues were clear to me: The husband was perverting the concept of submission to suit himself and hadn't the foggiest understanding of biblical love for his wife. But he wouldn't face the truth. It's easier to accept a doctor's diagnosis of flu than his discovery of cancer. The more blatant the demandingness (and here the analogy of flu breaks down because demandingness is lethal whether in subtle or blatant form), the less readily we tend to acknowledge it as wrong. The men who most arrogantly demand respect from their wives and children are the quickest to justify their style of leadership.

Most of us are a bit more subtle in our demanding ways and, I like to think, more open to calling them a problem once they're exposed. Admitting they are there and that they're sinful, however, is never easy, not even for the most mature. The inside look that brings about real change is unnerving, and it should be. The diagnosis of sin is not a pleasant one, and we tend to resist it whenever we can, preferring to think we've come farther than we have.

We simply must get to the core of the matter. The kind of change that most delights our Lord will never occur as long as we fuss only with sin in behavior or pain in the heart. Sin in the heart must be uncovered, looked at, and dealt with. When we understand we're thirsty people who foolishly go in wrong directions to find water, then we can look at our style of relating with an openness to recognizing a demanding, self-protective motive beneath our actions.

But we won't see these wrong directions on our own, any more than a coal miner will see where to dig without the help of a flashlight. Disciplined people won't recognize their protective (and unappealing) rigidity without help. Analytic types will fail to see that their cool logic, far from being admired, discourages those who would like to be close friends. Successful extroverts may go through life thinking everyone enjoys their social noise. Shy people may continue to regard themselves as quiet because of temperament and never see that their quietness is a protective cloak.

We need help to see ourself clearly. When we're serious about taking an inside look, God provides three sources of light:

1. The Spirit of God,
2. The Word of God,
3. The people of God.

Each resource can be used to replace the blindness of self-deceit with the clear vision of integrity.

The Spirit of God

The psalmist asked God to "Search me … and know my heart … See if there is any offensive way in me …" (Psalm 139:23-24).

I think I've heard more sermons about the *fullness* of the Spirit or the *indwelling* of the Spirit or the *sealing* of the Spirit or the *baptism* of the Spirit than I've heard about the *searching* of the Spirit. Each of the other topics provides reassurance and comfort. The searching work of God makes me uneasy.

But growth always requires discomfort. The Spirit was given not just to comfort but to convict (John 16:8). If our heart is the problem, and if it manages to hide its ugly contents beneath the covering of self-deceit, then the truth that God alone can see into our heart (Jeremiah 17:9-10) is a truth we must understand and apply. We must figure out how to let the Spirit of God make us aware of what He sees.

At this point, most discussions would turn to the art of meditation. And rightly so. We must not only read our Bible, listen to sermons, and explore spiritual matters with friends, but we must also find those quiet places, those still points in our hectic life when we are silent before God. Nothing restores perspective, provides refreshment, and reveals new direction quite as effectively as unhurried time with the Lord, time with no agenda and no purpose except communion. The Spirit of God can search us best when our soul is still.

But I don't think making time to hear God speak is a suggestion that gets to the core of things. There are deeper issues that interfere with the Spirit's searching ministry. Most of us hold to certain attitudes that send us running into the closet when He enters the room with His flashlight. Let me deal briefly with two

problems that can keep us from seeing ourselves clearly even during lengthy times of quiet retreat.

One problem is our focus. At precisely the moments we most
need to see ourself, we are often preoccupied with another's way
of treating us. It is difficult (and really seems rather nitpicky) to be
concerned about a slight crispness in my tone of voice toward a
friend who has spread vicious gossip about me.

The horrible truth is that our capacity for self-deceit can make
us believe that our problem is trivial compared to our friend's when
it's actually just as serious. In biblical language, the plank in our
own eye can feel like a speck while the speck in our friend's eye
looks like a plank. The reminder that we must focus on our own
responsibility may cause us to grudgingly look more closely at ourself, but we still think the other person is the real sinner.

If the Spirit of God is to do His work, we must shift our focus.
We must regularly invite Him to expose our own sin at exactly
those times we are least inclined to do so. No matter how griev-
ously we are sinned against and no matter how right it may be for
us to confront the sinner, *we must regard our tendency to respond
with a demand as a problem no less serious than the sin committed
against us.* "Search *me*, O God" is an appropriate prayer, especially
when we're reeling from the blow of another's sin.

A second obstacle to seeing ourself clearly is our goal. If it seems
unreasonable to ask God to search me when someone else is
blatantly wrong, then it certainly seems *unnecessary* to invite God's
probing look when everything is moving along pleasantly. What
is the point of beginning a vigorous exercise program if we're
enjoying good health and have no plans to run a marathon? No one
goes to the hospital for surgery if there are no symptoms of disease.

Most of us want our existence to be comfortable. We sleep on
the bed, not on the floor. Nothing is wrong with arranging for and
enjoying comfort—unless it becomes our highest priority. And
for many of us, perhaps most of us, it is. If we have little energy
or inclination to grapple with hard questions about our life, questions that arise when we measure ourself by the standards of holy
love, then it's likely our ultimate goal is not conformity to Christ
but comfort in this world.

My own life provides me with considerable comfort, much of which I have arranged for. I can see nothing wrong in warming the roll before I eat it. But I do find within me a frightening ability to relax in my pursuit of God when my life is going well. It sometimes seems to me that I already have what I *really* want— not the full riches of fellowship with God, but a close family, nice friends, enjoyable job, decent health, adequate bank account, and comfortable home. Although I prefer to think otherwise, the peaceful relaxation I sometimes feel may be more the product of temporal complacency that depends on immediate comfort than the fruit of resting in Christ's work and promise.

Complacency and rest are two very different things. Rest frees me from the anxious drivenness to live as I should, but it does not remove the passionate desire to know Christ better even when life is pleasant. The rest Christ provides entices me to know more of the One who provides it and to more eagerly want others to experience it.

The Christian who understands the sinfulness of his heart (not merely external sin and internal pain), and who appreciates the wonder of knowing God because he has tasted His goodness, will continue asking God to search him even when life is comfortable. Neither the sinfulness of others nor the comforts of life will weaken the maturing Christian's desire to know more of himself in order to clear away the obstacles to knowing more of God.

The pain of being sinned against makes the requirement to look at one's own sin seem unreasonable, even harsh. And the enjoyment of a pleasant life provides no impetus for such a look. Pain and comfort often keep us from being terribly interested in understanding our self-protective patterns. As a result, we don't often ask the Spirit of God to search us with a vengeance. But still He whispers convicting truth to people who are listening closely. The Spirit, I presume, is an able communicator. If we fail to hear what He says, it's because we're not paying attention. We may hear His voice (or think we do) telling us which job to take or which church to attend, but we rarely listen for His conviction of how we sinfully relate to others.

Because the Spirit's whispering is sometimes distorted as it passes through the defensive filters of our self-protective mind, we need more objective help in facing up to our demanding ways—help that is harder to ignore. The Word of God provides more direct input. And the people of God, when they function as they should, give feedback that requires sheer arrogance to disregard. Consider next the exposing function of Scripture.

The Word of God

Why is it that Christians spend years in the study of God's Word and remain unchanged where it counts, even hardened? Some, of course, do become increasingly loving, strong, and wise as they immerse themselves in Scripture, but many merely maintain their morals and orthodoxy. Others get more defensive, dogmatic, and distant. Why?

How can people hear the Bible taught in church Sunday after Sunday or study its contents in seminary classes for years and develop only a love for truth, a love that actually *removes them from people.*

Why do sincere believers rise early in the morning for time in the Word and then live their days with neither power in their ministry, peace in their struggles, nor love in their hearts? Why have many come to regard morning devotions as a lifeless ritual they either continue to practice out of habit or guilt—or simply abandon?

Surely the problem is not with the Bible. And the solution must never take us away from its appropriate use. But something is wrong when a sharp, two-edged sword glances off our skin without even drawing blood.

Perhaps it's time to screw up our courage and attack the sacred cow: We must admit that simply knowing the contents of the Bible is not a sure route to spiritual growth. There is an awful assumption in evangelical circles that if we can just get the Word of God into people's heads, then the Spirit of God will apply it to their hearts. That assumption is awful, not because the Spirit never does what the assumption supposes, but because it has excused pastors and leaders from the responsibility to tangle with people's lives. Many remain safely hidden behind pulpits, hopelessly out of touch with the struggles of their congregations, proclaiming the Scriptures with a pompous accuracy that touches no one. Pulpits should provide bridges, not barriers, to life-changing relationships.

Bible colleges and seminaries have spent enough time proving that merely instilling knowledge does not change lives. Graduates with impressive academic records have too often failed miserably in their ministries because of an inability to get along with others. Some have done everything well—preaching, administrating, raising money, visiting, evangelizing—but they haven't helped honest Christians deal effectively with the realities of their lives.

Paul could not have put the matter more clearly when he said, "Knowledge puffs up, but love builds up" (1 Corinthians 8:1). And yet so much of our reason for reading Scripture is to gain knowledge, and we're satisfied when we reach that goal.

A pastor friend told me that for years he'd never realized his wife was desperately lonely for relationship with him. He provided for her conscientiously, was thoughtful and kind, prayed with her regularly, and sincerely desired her well-being in every respect. One evening, when my wife and I were their guests for dinner, I was struck by how badly his shallow warmth was missing her, and offered a comment to that effect.

With an integrity typical of him, he puzzled over my observation until, weeks later, he concluded he'd never even thought about passionately pursuing relationship with his wife. He'd never felt his longings for intimacy keenly enough to motivate him toward richer involvement. He'd never recognized that his kindly spiritual style of relating was really protecting him from giving himself deeply to her—and facing the possibility of rejection.

In the next few months, his marriage took on a new vibrancy. His wife approached me one day with tears of joy and fear: "Things are so different. I've never felt so loved. Will it last?"

You must realize my friend was a committed Christian and a serious student of the Bible. I recently asked him how he understood Paul's teaching on marriage during all the years of their shallow relationship. He replied, "I never even dreamed Paul was telling me to really go after a relationship with my wife that required me to be real and to deeply touch her. I don't know why, but I never saw it that way."

The story is not uncommon: A man who could exegete the fifth chapter of Ephesians with scholarly precision missed its point. Knowledge of the text is not enough. It never is. Something more is required.

I must be careful to avoid an overreaction. The Bible still needs to be studied. It's wrong to handle a text like an authorized Ouija board. We are not to read a passage and expect the Spirit of God to mystically impress on our consciousness whatever self-knowledge He wants us to have. Biblical scholarship, whether practiced by highly trained specialists or by unschooled Christians who responsibly think through a text, provides the framework for all valid discussion of God's communication with His people. But scholarship is not the end point. Biblical scholarship may be more important than impressions but it's worth nothing if it doesn't eventually lead to personal impact. The text must affect our life and make us more loving, not just fill our head with more facts to support favorite doctrines.

It has often occurred to me that if God's intention was to present a body of truth merely to be intellectually grasped and then re-presented to others, He could have organized His one published work a little better. A group of scholars and prophets could have been assigned the job of preparing position papers on various topics, such as the work of the Holy Spirit, the doctrine of future events, or the purpose of the Law. We could then have an indexed manual with clear statements on all the key issues in orthodox Christianity. Think of the confusion such a book would have saved.

Granted, Paul did write a rather systematic treatise on the doctrine of salvation in his letter to the Romans, but even that was a personal letter, not a paper prepared for reading at a theology conference. The message was directed to people Paul wanted to instruct. It was not researched by a scholar in his study and then offered as a textbook to students who were intrigued by the subject.

The mood of the Bible is relational, personal. It's a book about people living their lives who recorded their God-ordered experiences and God-inspired wisdom for other people living their lives. To dissect its contents as a high school biology student dissects a frog, leaving its parts sitting in careful arrangement on the table, is a misuse of God's Word.

Study it, yes. Avail yourself of the valuable help scholars provide. Read commentaries. Take notes during sermons. Enroll in classes that require a scholarly study of the text. *But do it all for the purpose of better knowing God, yourself, and others so you become more loving.* Defending a millennial view in a style that contradicts love is damaging. Whatever we do with our Bible knowledge from within the walls of unchallenged self-protection has little real value. We must let Scripture penetrate to the thoughts and intents of our heart so we can more clearly see the ways we violate love. If we try to better understand God without taking a hard look at who we are, then our biblically derived knowledge of God will become mere theology, an assortment of correct but dull and lifeless facts. And if we try to figure out other people in order to reach them with God's truth without first working hard to understand ourselves, we'll fail to recognize in them what we do not see in ourselves (Matthew 7:1-5).

What I've said so far about the importance of a lively approach to Scripture seems to me to be reasonably clear. But as I prepare to write the next few pages, I realize it's easier to talk about the *value* of using the Bible to understand us than to lay out the *method* for doing so. I'm tempted to repeat some worthwhile but obvious suggestions about dividing the time we spend in the Word into a period for study and a period for meditation. Perhaps a long walk away from the library or an occasional afternoon or weekend set aside for the explicit purpose of pondering our life in the light of certain passages would help. Times of stillness are as vital as they are rare. We need quiet moments to read the story of Samson and wonder how we are like him in stubbornly pursuing whatever catches our fancy. Yet we can sincerely devote chunks of time to thinking through our life and come away bored, unchallenged, and—worst of all—unpenetrated by the sword. All Scripture is useful for teaching, rebuking, correcting, and training in righteousness (2 Timothy 3:16), so our time in the Bible should cut through our protective armor to expose the arrogant fear that keeps us looking out for ourself more than trusting God. It should reach deeply into our heart where the core problems lie.

What can we do to encourage that work to happen more often and more fully? Part of the answer is really quite simple: *We must come to the Bible with the purpose of self-exposure consciously in mind.* I suspect not many people make more than a token stab in that direction. It's extremely hard work. It makes Bible study alternately convicting and reassuring, painful and soothing, puzzling and calming, and sometimes dull—but not for long if our purpose is to see ourself better.

The Bible comes alive for me with penetrating impact at unpredictable times. More than once I've reached for my Bible with the definite purpose of seeing myself more clearly and have found a deep comfort that kept me still in the midst of a stormy conflict. At other times I've been troubled over tensions in an important relationship, gone to the Bible looking for wisdom to handle things well—and come away with nothing. At still other times, the teaching in a certain text or the example of a biblical character has pulled back the curtains to let some light shine on my situation, giving me direction for improving my response. The Bible is not a vending machine that reliably yields the product we request.

A humble attitude of dependence expressed in the conscious goal of self-exposure gets us asking the right questions as we read our Bible. Rather than wagging our head and admitting with noble self-deprecation, "Ah, yes, there are times I'm just like Samson, preferring my own sensual comfort to the things of God," we can be seized by the narrative with conviction that leads to change. But we must ask the questions that lead to conviction, questions such as: What must have been going on in Samson's head to make him disregard his high calling and go against his parents' wishes? What within him supplied the energy for sinning so recklessly? What satisfaction was provided by the prospects of a relationship with the Philistine woman? Was Manoah's lament that he and his wife were doomed to die because they'd seen God the evidence of an alarmist tendency his wife needed to balance with her sensible reassurance (Judges 13:22-23)?

We tend to ask the "right" questions (the ones that lead to personal impact) only when we approach the text in order to see ourself more clearly. That is the first condition necessary if the Sword is to penetrate our soul. A second condition is equally important. We must also understand the basics of how people function. A biblical view of people requires us to think about those parts of our soul that pant after God as well as the deceitful foolishness that leads us away from Him. As we ponder the record of Samson's life in light of the deep longings of his soul and the sinful strategies of his deceitful heart, destructive patterns in our own life that parallel those in Samson's will eventually surface.

We must read the New Testament epistles with the same attitude and goal. If we're aware of our potential for relationship and for its violation, Paul's teaching on marriage can provoke deep thought and right questions. His command that husbands love their wives should lead to reflection on what exactly a woman desires from a man and on a man's inclination to respond less to her desires and more to his own desire to feel macho.

As we sincerely commit ourself to the purpose of self-exposure and realize that the people in the Bible are longing beings and self-protective demanders just like us, we might be able to stand still under the spotlight of Scripture and let it do its work. If we study the text merely to learn truth, failing to hear the heartbeat of real people as they live before us in the Bible, then our time in the Word will lead to superficial change at best. When we miss the personalness of Scripture and come to it without the integrity that desires exposure, the lamp to our feet and the light to our path is dimmed.

The Spirit can be quenched and the Word can be intellectualized. Fortunately, there is a third resource for seeing ourself that can have an impact more difficult to ignore.

The People of God

I can think of nothing more important for spiritual growth than good relationships in the Body of Christ. Several books have been written about the "one-anothering" commands of Scripture: love one another, bear one another's burdens, rejoice and weep with

one another, and so on. But an important part of our responsibility to fellow Christians has been neglected: *to give feedback lov-*
ingly and *to receive feedback non-defensively.*

We have not taken the truth that our heart is deceitful seriously enough. We can, with unfeigned sincerity, believe we are
doing quite well spiritually while our style of relating to significant people is more self-protective than loving. We are like a child
cleaning his room under orders. When the bed is made (or at least
some effort has been given to the task) and when the clothes are
off the floor and out of sight, he pronounces the room clean. A
surface tidiness is all that's needed. Until mother comes. One look
beneath the wrinkled bed is enough to send her howling after
Johnny. When the hidden mess is exposed, Johnny looks puzzled,
almost hurt by his mother's critical reaction. "You wanted me to
clean that up, too?"

We really do need help in establishing standards of cleanliness
and then seeing where we don't measure up. If the Word of God
presents the ideal and the Spirit of God pulls away the bedspread
to expose the work yet to be done, then perhaps the people of God
can put the finger on specific concerns that need attention.

We are warned to "see to it ... that none of you has a sinful,
unbelieving heart that turns away from the living God" (Hebrews
3:12). But our heart is inclined toward sin and unbelief, and worse,
it cleverly deceives us into thinking it's healthy when it's not.
Therefore, the writer to the Hebrews quickly follows his warning
against a sinful heart with the admonition to "encourage one
another daily, as long as it is called Today, so that none of you may
be hardened by sin's deceitfulness" (Hebrews 3:13).

Apparently we are to interact with one another on a daily
basis in ways that help us see how our sinful hearts tend to operate. I take it that my responsibility is to know a few people well
enough to form some ideas about the specific ways, both obvious and subtle, in which they violate the command to love. And
I am to allow myself in daily relationships to be known in the
same way.

Certainly when sin above the waterline occurs, when someone
clearly contradicts God's holy standards by committing adultery

or cheating in business, we are to confront the offending person in a humble spirit of restoration. But most of our efforts to deal with each other's sinfulness are directed at that sort of overt sin, or perhaps at straightening out obvious tensions in a relationship. The subtleties of self-protective sin, the ways in which our determination to stay out of pain lead us to compromise our calling to be involved with others, go unnoticed and unaddressed. And yet these patterns of self-protection are tragic because they keep people from relating with power. Groups of cordial folks who get along well and enjoy one another's company may study the Scriptures and pray together, but most of the members know they haven't been touched. Encouraged, perhaps, instructed, but not changed into people who powerfully penetrate others with the dynamic of Christian reality.

Christians have only two options when it comes to forming relationships: either remain comfortably distant from the struggles and sinfulness in one another or open a can of worms. When the first option is selected, church life goes on as usual: warm, polite, enjoyable, orthodox, occasionally disrupted by someone's terrible sin, but generally irrelevant to central parts of people's lives. When the second option is chosen, the group may at times seem more disruptive than helpful. Some members will become dejected, wondering whatever happened to encouragement. Others will be offended and change churches. But when the worms of self-protection and demandingness are let out of the can, when people get to know each other's hurts and disappointments, when issues that really matter are actually talked about, then there is the potential for life-changing fellowship.

Obviously, I am vigorously contending for the second option. But not without concern. Communicating about real problems in our life doesn't ensure encouragement from others. Too often, people who become vulnerable end up feeling misunderstood, embarrassed, burdensome, or hopeless because of their struggles. And yet the thousand ways to ruin a marriage do not present a good argument for singleness. Groups that look at lives honestly have the potential to divide and destroy, but they also have the power to bless. The risk is worth it, but more importantly, the risk is commanded. We are told to relate in a way that keeps us from becoming hardened by the deceitfulness of sin.

Observing a few cautions might help us realize the good potential of honest fellowship and minimize some of its danger. First, *remember that honest sharing is not the final goal*. Love is. There are times when telling you what's on my mind has nothing whatsoever to do with concern for your well-being. In the development of a relationship, much needs to be left unsaid. Love will restrain me from saying what I judge may hurt you needlessly. Sharing must be limited not by self-protection but by sensitive love.

Second, *good fellowship is characterized by support and kindness, not by confrontation*. We are not to gather together for the purpose of spotting somebody's sin. If the mood of a group seems defensive, irritable, or cool, look to see if more attention is being given to exposing sinful strategies than to understanding deep longings. On the other hand, if the mood is congenial and warm but somehow empty, perhaps the group members are afraid to honestly discuss issues of self-protection in one another.

Healthy group dynamics don't happen automatically, they grow in the rich soil of time, prayer, and trust. Groups that meet to promote inside-out change among their members would do well to engage in light conversation over meals, set aside times for sheer fun, and draw together in prayer and worship. A context of warmth and support with a clearly acknowledged spiritual framework is essential to the proper functioning of a group that deals with the threatening issues of self-protection.

Third, *meaningful involvement must precede efforts to expose each other's sin*. The level of involvement, both past and anticipated, determines the level of exposure. In a local church, I can be involved with only a handful of people at a level that warrants blunt interaction about each other's defensive patterns. No one should appoint himself Minister of Exposure to the entire congregation. When someone tells me I come across as pushy, my ability to receive that input well depends partly on how persuaded I am that the one who's given the input genuinely cares about me. Someone who *enjoys* providing critical feedback is not qualified to do so. His enjoyment betrays his purpose in giving feedback as more self-protective than loving.

With these cautions in mind, we must pray for and actively seek an ongoing opportunity to talk honestly about our life and the lives of others, not settling for what sometimes passes for discipleship where people learn about truth but never deal directly with what's going on in their relationships. With requested direction from God's Spirit and with God's Word as a guiding framework for discussion, Christians who gather with the express purpose of looking at their lives together can expect good things to happen.

Each member of the group needs to understand its *purpose*. Sunday school classes meet to receive systematic instruction from the Bible. Christians attend preaching services to be taught and inspired by God's Word. Some small groups meet for further Bible study or to organize a specific ministry or to enjoy fellowship. But people who come to the kind of group I'm describing must know their purpose is to speak the truth in love about what they observe in others in order to help each other develop styles of relating that are less cluttered with self-protection. That purpose, however, will not be realized without a generally accepted *framework* for understanding people. In my view, some discussion of the two ideas of deep longings and self-protection can provide a way of looking at each other's lives that can in turn spark insightful conversations.

Not only does the group need a purpose and a framework, it also needs a *method*, one that's flexible enough to bend to whatever good direction a particular evening takes and structured enough to keep things together when very little is happening. Perhaps a traditional study of a particular book of the Bible would provide a useful format. Listening to a tape series or discussing topics like "What do I tend to avoid?" or "What do I know about the joys of personal intimacy?" might be good alternatives. Or maybe group members would benefit from sharing their history up to the present, including significant disappointments and joys, in order to better understand deep longings that are satisfied or frustrated as well as sinful strategies that need attention. The core method is not so much the planned format as it is the *commitment to evaluate what happens as the group interacts.*

In a group I'm part of, a woman seemed to consistently "rescue" her husband. She had requested the group's help in controlling expressions of anger toward her children. One member asked whether her husband was strongly involved with the kids and how he reacted to her inappropriate anger. "Well," she replied, "he really isn't with the kids as much as I am; he works late most evenings. And when he is there and I lose my temper at one of our children, he just kind of glares at me. But he really is a good father and I know he loves me and the kids."

After hearing her repeat something like "but he really is a good father" many times over several weeks, someone pointed out her pattern of defending her husband from her own attacks.[1] That comment opened the door for her to see that she was refusing to deal honestly with how angry she was and how deeply she felt he had let her down.

A new level of communication developed for the couple as each of them began to admit their hurt and the strategies they were using to run from it. They are learning to trust the Lord more deeply with their thirst and to move toward one another in nondefensive commitment. The road has been rocky, but their marriage is now filled with more warmth and genuine caring than they had known in their previous sixteen years of marriage.

Small groups need a purpose, a framework, a method, and finally, a *leader*, or at least an organizer. Credentials for leadership include *personal integrity* (a willingness to look deeply inside one's own life), *compassionate sensitivity* (a character quality that develops by facing one's own pain and learning to commit it to the Lord), and *some awareness of how people function*.

If you have a burden to relate at a deeper level, to give and receive honest feedback that leads to supportive and encouraging fellowship, then talk to a few people who might share your interest. Explain your idea to them and discuss the purpose, framework, and method of a possible small group. If a handful seem to get excited, schedule your first meeting. Then go slowly. Don't push people into "honest" interaction. Be more sensitive to longings than to strategies, at least initially. Explain the framework in enough detail to stimulate people to think carefully about their lives.

Enjoy good times together: play, eat, chat, worship, pray, study. Allow the group time to develop a comfortable anticipation of being together. Suggest after perhaps several months (it could be much sooner or much later) that the group move to a more open level of interacting. If there is resistance, explore it gently and honor it if it continues. Don't try to make things happen at the pace you want. Wait. Pray.

Eventually you'll have the opportunity to shift the group into higher gear. Start by asking for feedback about yourself: "I think I have a hard time getting really close to people. I've wondered if I communicate that I'm too busy or too important for real friendship. I'd appreciate hearing how each of you experiences me in this group, even right now as I share this. How do I make you feel?"

Remember that shifting the conversation about things in the Bible or events from last week to *what is going on right now between group members* is extremely difficult. It can be as traumatic as shelving an often-read book about marriage and actually asking a girl to marry you. Expect discomfort in yourself and others. Some may drop out of the group. Perhaps you moved too fast. Perhaps not. You won't always know. Accept the confusion and disappointment and press on.

Some may share their dissatisfaction with the way the group is handled, particularly by you. Explore their attitudes and feelings. You may get into a few defensive and even angry conversations. Keep in mind that the road to relationship is never smooth. Your only option is to retreat to polite conversation that touches no one deeply. Count the cost, then go for it. Be patient, but persevere. Learning about ourself through intense interaction with fellow believers provides an incomparable opportunity to grow. God's Spirit and God's Word are crucial, but the power of God's people must not be underrated. The three-legged stool is not very sturdy when it has only two legs.

The Spirit of God, the Word of God, and the people of God: three sources of help in learning about our sinful strategies of self-protection. Awareness of thirst must come first; then, recognition of self-protection. Finally, we must do something about the thirst and sin an inside look uncovers.

So far, we've thought about the ways in which our thirst drives us to dig broken cisterns. Now it's time to see how we can stop digging, put down our shovels, and learn to drink deeply from the well of living water.

Notes

1. I believe the ability to recognize that pattern depends less on counseling than on a nondefensive concern for other people *and* an openness to facing similar problems in oneself.

CHAPTER TEN

DEFINING THE PROBLEM

In our efforts to change, no question is more important than the obvious one: *What exactly is wrong?* What is going on in us that leads to depression, worry, sexual perversion, hostility, and a host of other concerns that plague us? Is there something tucked away in our deceitful heart that a sincere commitment to follow Christ and renewed determination to live as we should simply do not reach? Do most counseling efforts miss a central problem that must be corrected if change from the inside out is to occur?

Problems are everywhere: single parents struggling to be both mom and dad, wives drying up as women in marriages to hopelessly weak husbands, men battling occasionally overwhelming urges to look at pornographic literature, teenagers torn apart by feelings of resentment toward parents they love.

Sometimes the reality of human suffering seems just too much. Everyone has his or her story to tell. When I reach my limit, when I've heard enough, then a friend confides in me a burden I never suspected he carries, and my jaded complacency shatters into an almost desperate cry that God do more than He seems to be doing.

Perhaps my viewpoint is distorted by my profession, like a specialist who treats cancer patients every day and forgets that some people are healthy. But when I have the opportunity to speak intimately with my "healthy" friends, I usually discover either that their lives are not as together as they appear or that they've preserved pleasantness by sacrificing depth in their self-awareness and relationships with others.

Christians must remember we live in a fallen world. That truth has enormously important implications. Something really is wrong with everything. We should expect, therefore, that an honest look at both our life and others' will uncover significant problems.

Our response to the mess need not be discouraged retreat, cynical non-involvement, or a shallow pursuit of personal comfort. We need not throw up our hands in defeat and glumly live out our days. Escaping into arrogantly elite conversations with other enlightened folk who know better than to work at improving things is not the answer. Neither is sealing ourselves away from troubling reality by distracting ourself with television, busyness, pleasant friendships, and enjoyable religion. We are called to enter the disturbing realities of our own life and the lives of others with life-changing truth.

But there's the rub. The truth we embrace and the principles we try to follow don't seem to be changing very many people. Perhaps they keep us going, but not with the deep vitality that draws others. We manage to get ourself rearranged and held together to look like a person who's living for God, but we know something inside is very different from what the Bible tells us can be there. Something is missing. Something is wrong. And we know it. Like the patient who carefully follows doctor's orders but continues to feel the pain that brought him in for treatment, we worry (properly) that a serious problem is not being cured by the prescribed medication.

If an inside look is to be profitable, it must begin with a clear definition of the central problem that needs changing. What is it? What is the dirt on the inside of the cup and dish that must be exposed and scoured off? Our temper? Lack of self-control? Traumatic memories from childhood? Insincere commitment? Deep insecurity? Psychological disease? Poorly handled temperament? Self-pity? Biblical ignorance? Laziness? Negative self-talk?

Stubborn sinfulness? Meaninglessness? What must we deal with if we are to be changed substantially and progressively until we die? What problem needs correction in order for change to take place from the inside out?

When we clearly identify the problem, then and only then will we come to deeply appreciate the solution. The more fully we comprehend the ugliness of sin, the more lovely the Cross of Christ becomes. The concluding section of this book attempts first to define the problem (chapter 10) and then to present the pathway to real change (chapters 11 and 12).

Facing Our Sin

As I prepare to take up the subject of what needs changing and how deep change can occur, three preliminary thoughts come to mind. First, some readers may by now be feeling impatient. "Okay, so I admit I don't have everything I want—my deep longings are not fully satisfied. And I see that I sometimes work hard to feel good anyhow, which I guess is self-protective. But I'm still not sure what you think I ought to do to get over my problems."

I suspect some are wondering when I intend to wrap up my theorizing and get to something practical. Let me say it gently: There is nothing theoretical about entering our pain and facing our sin. People who ask, "So now what do I do?" generally are still walking around the edges of their disappointment, perhaps admitting that life has had its share of hurts, but working hard (often unconsciously) to blunt their feelings of sadness with a stoical let's-get-on-with-it attitude.

It's doubtful these impatient, practical folks are terribly aware of their sin. Adultery, lying, theological compromise—these are the sins they concern themselves with, sins of which they (conveniently) are innocent. Self-protection is a category of sin they don't consider. And if they do look at their self-protective sin, it seems quite reasonable to them. Very few people ever recognize how ugly it is to not love, especially when the failure is subtle.

As we try to understand the process of change, we must realize that deep change comes about less because of what we try to do and how hard we try to do it, and more because of *our will-ingness to face the realities of our own internal life*. Personal integrity, a commitment to never pretend about anything, is prerequisite for change from the inside out.

That commitment is tough to honor. When the fullness of our disappointment drives us to an overwhelming sorrow that replaces anger with pain, when we can feel in our stomach how badly we wanted our father to be there and our mother to non-possessively care, we will be shaken to the core of our being. That kind of pain, I submit, is the starting point for real change. It is only when we face the horror of desperately longing for what no one has or ever will provide that we give up our demands of others to satisfy our thirst and we turn in humble, broken dependence to God.

Most of us have memories we won't think about—painful moments with a parent that may seem trivial till we reflect on them, wrenching episodes of sexual or emotional abuse. Ignoring past pain sometimes seems like the only logical thing to do, yet pockets of angry rage stay hidden in our soul. To deny we're hungry after days without food and that we feel anger toward people who could have fed us but refused is not evidence of maturity. Christians starving during a famine feel just as hungry as unfed pagans. It's right to admit we're hungry and normal to look for food to satisfy us. But to admit hunger and then look for food to give to those who earlier withheld it is not normal, it is Christian. And we can't do it without passionate confidence in the Bread of heaven who sustains us with manna now but promises a banquet later.

When we face how deeply disappointed we are with our rela-tionships, it then becomes possible to recognize the ugliness of what before seemed reasonable. When I realize how badly I want someone to come through for me in a way no one has, then (and not until then) can I see how hard I work either to get what I want or to protect myself from the anguish of more disappointment.

The painful awareness of disappointment that leads to the con-victing recognition of self-protective sin is the framework within which real change can take place. The impatient desire to get "prac-tical" advice for solving life's problems often reflects an effort to bypass the pain of an inside look. When that look is avoided, when we fail to face our deep disappointment and relational sin, then the best we can manage is superficial change. Most advice on things to do heals the wound of God's people as though it were not serious (Jeremiah 6:14).

Embracing the Mystery

The second thought that comes to mind as I consider how deep change can occur is that the process of change will always, to some degree, remain a mystery. As I collect my ideas about change, I'm tempted to talk more about what confuses me than what I think I understand. But that would lead to an intolerably long book, perhaps several volumes. Better to discuss what seems somewhat clear and keep it short. People who proclaim a message of change that "represents a breakthrough in our knowledge and is guaranteed to revolutionize your life" (or change your marriage or make your kids lovable or replace depression with pep) make me think of Paul's words: "The man who thinks he knows something does not yet know as he ought to know" (1 Corinthians 8:2). Apparently true knowledge produces a humility that keeps us open to more thinking.

I do not want to communicate an attitude of "Okay, here is the answer you've been waiting for. Forget all your preacher or counselor has been telling you. This is what Christianity is all about. This is the biblical route to change." I do think I have something to say or I wouldn't be writing a book. And I believe my understanding of change emerges from Scripture and will prove helpful. But I want to present my thinking with a clear recognition that even the clearest model (a claim I am not making for this book) will not eliminate mystery.

To insist we judge our theories in terms of their "biblicalness" is, of course, a proper thing to do, but it is not without its problems. The fact that conservative scholars seem to differ on every theological issue except a few essential doctrines makes me hesitate to confidently declare any one position on change as biblical or unbiblical. Yet some people's ideas strike me immediately as shallow. Others analyze how their own lives have been changed and offer that process as normative, replacing the authority of Scripture with personal experience. Still others seem to come up with a model that uniquely fits their style of relating. Aggressive, let's-get-on-with-it types prefer a theory of change that pushes people to be different. Quiet, warm folks are drawn to an understanding of change that emphasizes empathetic concern as a context for growth.

My question as I evaluate the models of change is whether they produce Christlike *character* or Christlike *behavior*. Does a certain model endorse obedience and trust as the route to producing realness, humility, and a richer sense of being alive? Or does it tend to shape people into the likeness of a Christian (according to someone's ideas about how a Christian should look) without developing within them that powerful and liberating vitality that is at once threatening and attractive?

So many people who glowingly report that their lives have been turned around by a seminar, a church, or a counselor sometimes make me think of figures in a wax museum. They look like the real thing, but they don't breathe. You expect them to move like living people, but they never do. These are not the folks you want to be with when you're in real trouble or deep pain. Their words of encouragement are always appropriate and warmly offered, but they fall flat. You never feel more alive after a conversation with them—a bit cheered or instructed, perhaps, but never alive.

Developing the spark that is the unmistakable evidence of life is the challenge before us—and also the mystery. Techniques, theories, formulas, discipline, knowledge, commitment—nothing quite adds up to equal life. The lamp for our path illumines our next step but leaves much ahead, beside, and behind in darkness. Change from the inside out will always be, in the final analysis, a work of God, and must therefore remain a mystery. Remembering this can help us keep realistic expectations of any teaching on change as well as reverence for the God whose ways are far above ours.

Accepting the Process

A third point about change from the inside out is that it's a process. Unlike surgery, where the doctor can sometimes remove the offending tissue and send us home with a clean bill of health, ongoing change takes a lifetime. We are wrong to be surprised when we (or others) react with sinful immaturity.

Too often, we expect a dramatic moment of profound commitment or stirring worship to change us forever. When we return to our familiar level of boredom or drivenness or impatience, it's easy to become very disillusioned. Will we never change? A complacency that takes sin lightly is wrong, but an internal comfort that allows us to press on after failure is a legacy of the Cross. Christ's sacrificial death allows us to accept our enduring sinfulness. There is always more to deal with.

Perhaps my greatest personal concern as I write this book comes from those times when I feel so woefully unchanged. Have the concepts I write about been changing my life? More than once, I've put down my pen, feeling utterly unqualified to teach anyone else how to change. And yet I believe growth in my life is visible. There are times when the evidence of God's work in my heart absolutely thrills me. Other times, if I didn't understand that salvation is an unearned gift, I'd be tempted to question my spiritual standing.

The process of change is something like a walk across America. Every step is progress but there's such a long way to go. The trick is to be encouraged with how far you've come without letting pride weaken your determination to continue on. An honest look at the distance yet to be covered should cure the most advanced saint of conceit.

As we take a more specific look at how to change, keep in mind my introductory points. First, awareness of all that's within us is more important to changing than a set of instructions about what to believe and do. Second, the actual process of change can never be fully explained; the work of God's Spirit cannot be packaged into our neat categories. We must expect neither precision in our understanding of change nor confidence that we're saying all that needs to be said. Third, no one is fully changed. It should comfort us to know that everyone has ample room to grow. Even Paul admitted, "I do not consider myself yet to have taken hold of it" (Philippians 3:13), referring to the richness of all Christ has provided.

Identifying Problem Areas

Consider the plight of a woman married to a weak, uninvolved husband. She is aware of chronic resentment toward him and an emptiness that gnaws at her soul. When he approaches her for sex (which he rarely does), she finds nothing in her that wants to respond or cooperate. Efforts to communicate typically cause him to retreat even further. Counsel to "build him up" or to "tell him how you really feel" or to "be vulnerable and trust God for the results" seems pointless. She's feeling desperate. She finds little enjoyment in being a woman. Her feelings of depression are becoming harder to ignore or to overcome with distracting busyness. The situation is further complicated by the subtle but clear advances of her husband's business associate. Although she's a Christian woman who wants to live by biblical standards, she's frightened by her growing attraction to this man.

As she thinks through her dilemma, she identifies three categories of problems. One, *problems in her world.* A weak husband heads the list. If he would come alive as a man and lovingly take hold of their relationship, it could rekindle her love. Two, *pain in her heart.* She is aware of rage, disappointment, emptiness, and guilt over both her disgust with her husband and her attraction to the other man. Three, *sin in her behavior.* She knows her coldness toward her husband isn't helping the situation. And she struggles against the temptation to pursue an illicit relationship with someone she finds more desirable than him.

The intensity of her problems makes her determined to do something about them. She's miserably unhappy and knows she's walking close to the edge of moral compromise. She wants to do what she can to change things. With her problems divided into three categories, she decides to cover all bases.

She approaches her pastor, asking him to talk with her husband. Together they agree to pray that God will convince him of his responsibility to strongly love her. Direct intervention and prayer are aimed at the problems in her world (category 1). She schedules to see a professional counselor to "work through" the chaos of internal emotions that threaten to undo her. She hopes counseling will help her deal with the pain in her heart (category 2). In conversation with both her pastor and her counselor, she seeks advice on the best way to respond to her husband. She wants to obey the biblical command to submit but is confused about what that requires of her in certain situations. As she thinks through her responsibilities, she determines to spend more time in Bible reading and church activities to strengthen her against sin in her behavior (category 3).

Months go by. She comes to understand her struggles better. In counseling, she begins to see that her father was weak and passive like her husband. The intensity of her rage in the present, her counselor explains, reflects unresolved anger from her past. She feels less confused about her internal reactions, but she still hurts. With the support of both pastor and counselor, she decides to take hold of her life rather than give in to self-defeating bitterness and sulking. She takes on a part-time job, joins a tennis league, and volunteers to help with the children during junior church services.

Neither her pastor nor counselor has been able to influence her husband. He continues to be pleasant but entirely uninvolved, and she continues to hurt when she thinks about her marriage. She does her best to be friendly and cooperate with his desires. His reaction to her kindness is the strengthened assumption that everything is back to normal. Although that makes her furious, she works to control herself and trust the Lord while she continues to be kind. She still wrestles with her attraction to her husband's colleague, but lives with a day-by-day commitment to avoid any wrong encounter.

In many Christian circles, that outcome, given her husband's refusal to change, would be regarded as good. Some might question the value of self-understanding through counseling, assuming that being kinder to her husband and more involved with church and productive activities has been the real source of help. But most would be delighted with her renewed commitment to serve the Lord. That commitment, many would say, is evidence of God's work in her heart.

But the heart is deceitful. In order to have a "right heart," we must understand and deal with its capacity for subtle sin. In addition to problems in our world, pain in our heart, and sin in our behavior, we must acknowledge a fourth problem category: *sin in our heart.*

We are both *victims* of our world and *agents* in it. As longing people who thirst for what this world can never provide, we have all suffered disappointment. We have been hurt by others. We are victims whenever we are sinned against or whenever we suffer in any way without cause. But we are also agents, choosing to respond to life according to our understanding of what is best. Because we're foolishly determined to arrange for our own gratification, we refuse to believe God and to trust Him with our longings in a way that frees us to deeply love others.

We are disappointed as victims and culpable as agents. We have been sinned against, and we continue to be injured by others' sin. But we have also sinned, and we continue to work at preserving our life with defensive patterns of relating. The disappointment we suffer comes from *problems in our world* that create *pain in our heart.* Our culpability shows itself when we *sin in our behavior* as a result of the *sin in our heart.*

What Needs to Be Changed?

Perhaps these four categories and their interrelationships will become clearer if we return to our sketch of two icebergs. Let our deep longings be one iceberg, with the longings for change in our world represented above the waterline and longings only Christ can satisfy represented below the waterline. Let the other iceberg depict our wrong strategies for relating to others, with our visible acts of disobedience sketched above the waterline and our self-protective motives hidden beneath it. The waterline itself represents our conscious awareness. Issues we do not clearly recognize within ourself fall beneath that line. As we take an inside look with the help of the Word, Spirit, and people of God, we lower the water-line and become more aware of our longings and our sin.

The four categories of problems can be sketched this way:

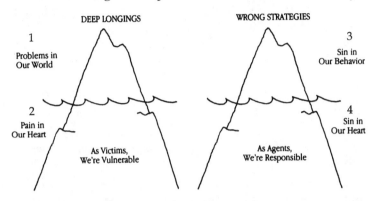

Where in the sketch can we locate our central problem? Where is the dirt that must be scoured away if we are to change from the inside out?

Problems in our world will continue until we die. Our Lord told us clearly that "in this world you will have trouble" (John 16:33). James instructs us to "consider it pure joy ... whenever you face trials of many kinds" (James 1:2). Problems in our world are not the source of a disordered, unhappy life. They do not define the dirt.

Pain in our heart can be very real and thoroughly exhausting. But Peter, in speaking to a group of persecuted Christians, does not scold them for their pain. Instead, he offers the hope of "inexpressible and glorious joy" (1 Peter 1:8), as they contemplate the salvation that is their guarantee. We tend to make the relief of our pain a goal. Meditation techniques, healing bad memories, and catharsis of internal struggles are procedures designed to deal with our pain directly. But the pain isn't the dirt. It's only a source of discomfort with which our Lord sympathizes.

The inside dirt that must be scoured away if there is to be inside-out change is not the pain of disappointment we suffer as victims; it is the filth of sin and rebellion we choose as agents. *Deep change requires that we correct problems arising from our responsibility to choose, not those resulting from our vulnerability to be disappointed.*

Sin in our behavior clearly is a problem we must deal with. The immoral man in the Corinthian church was required to pay a severe price for committing blatant sin. But when Paul gave instructions for handling that man, his intent was to do more than put a stop to his sinful behavior. He recommended that the church take strong action "so that the sinful nature may be destroyed" (1 Corinthians 5:5).

Sins in behavior are certainly a problem, but they are symptoms of a deeper problem. "Listen and understand," said our Lord. "What goes into a man's mouth does not make him 'unclean,' but what comes out of his mouth, that is what makes him 'unclean' " (Matthew 15:10-11).

When He explained this teaching to His disciples through a parable, they missed the point. Peter said, "Explain the parable to us."

"Are you still so dull?" Jesus asked them. "Don't you see that whatever enters the mouth goes into the stomach and then out of the body? But the things that come out of the mouth come from the heart, and these make a man 'unclean.' For out of the heart come evil thoughts, murder, adultery, sexual immorality, theft, false testimony, slander. These are what make a man 'unclean' " (Matthew 15:15-20).

The fourth category of concern, *sin in our heart*, is where we must look to find the dirt that needs cleansing. We must not brush aside the seriousness of our heart problems by agreeing that, "Well, of course our heart has to be right." For most people, that means nothing more than a consciously sincere commitment to follow the Lord. And that is, of course, a good and necessary beginning. But more is required. Because our heart is deceitful, we don't naturally recognize the core sin in our heart that must be dealt with through repentance. Most efforts to change focus on one or more of the other three categories of problems and deal only superficially with sin in our heart.

I believe there's a simple reason why sin in the heart, that commitment to self-protection that manifests itself in so many defensive styles of relating, is so rarely recognized as deep and serious. We can't recognize self-protection until we see what we're protecting. Until we face our disappointment as a victim, we cannot clearly identify the strategies we've adopted to insulate ourself from further disappointment. *Only a deep awareness of our own profound disappointment (pain in our heart) can enable us to realize our desires for satisfaction have become demands for relief (sin in our heart).* Although we may define the problem of self-protection, we won't *identify* the problem in our own life until we're in touch with the damage to our soul caused by other people's sinfulness, a painful damage that motivates our self-protection in the first place.

Change from the inside out is rare. Very few people are willing to deeply embrace their disappointment. And even fewer, when they've faced their disappointment and are filled with excruciating pain and sadness, are willing to firmly say, "My pain is not the problem. The problem is my determination to relieve my pain any way I can."

To call self-protection the problem right at the moment when the pain is most severe is not easy. But it must be done. When relieving pain becomes our priority, then we have left the path of pursuing God. The experience of pain has the power to either harden us in our self-protective style or to drive us to deeper trust in God. It can enable us to clearly see how our relational style accommodates our commitment to stay safe rather than to freely love others. Self-protection and love are opposites. Since love is the ultimate virtue, self-protection is the ultimate problem.

The woman whose husband is weak needs to do more than pray about the problems in her world, try to understand the pain in her heart, and work to resist obvious sin in her behavior. She must face the pain in her soul until her anger is overwhelmed with a desperate sorrow. She must then examine her life to see pervasive patterns of self-protection. As she's convicted of the sinfulness of her failure to love, she must repent and bring forth the fruits of repentance. Repentance is the key. The last two chapters of this book are devoted to exploring what it means to repent of sin in our heart.

The Value of Entering Our Disappointment

An important point in this chapter must not be overlooked: Before we'll see how sinful we are as a self-protective agent, we must first feel how disappointed we are as a vulnerable victim. Let me illustrate what I mean.

I belong to a small group that gathers for the explicit purpose of providing honest, loving feedback to one another. One evening, a member of our group told his story. He began by rejoicing in the observation that he was feeling compassion for others far more deeply than ever before. When people interrupted his work, he was sometimes delighted with the opportunity to relate. In the past, he'd felt offended by the obstacle to progress in his work. But still, he confessed, he did not sense an ability within him to deeply penetrate other people. This is a man I respect. He is a strong Christian who understands what it means to trust the Lord in difficult times. And yet he knew something was wrong with the quality of his relationships.

We encouraged him to ramble about his upbringing, focusing on times of disappointment and his means of handling it. As he related to us some rather awful stories about a domineering mother who mercilessly overprotected him and a weak father who never dealt with his wife's blatant possessiveness, I was struck by the absence of any real feeling. Except for a few moments when anger crept into his voice, he could just as easily have been reading names from a phone book.

At one point, another member commented with some passion, "You were badly betrayed by your father and wrongly owned by your mother." "Yes, that's true," he replied, still with little emotion in his voice.

The theme of our feedback became his refusal to enter deeply into the experience of his disappointment. With uncharacteristic defensiveness (this man normally exhibits unusual integrity) he responded to our feedback by claiming he knew how badly he'd been failed but could not see any value in letting himself become consumed with his pain.

"Am I to focus on my pain and think about nothing other than how badly I've been victimized? I'm more interested in knowing how I can get on with my life. What's past is past. I want to learn to relate effectively to people now."

But the problem blocking his effective relating in the present was not a lack of knowledge, skill, or willpower. It was his self-protective commitment to never experience the level of pain he'd felt in his childhood and many times since. He had learned to dutifully obey his mother. He didn't dare warmly share his heart with her; she would have swallowed him even more with her absorbing possessiveness. Matter-of-fact obedience with occasional bursts of anger was his safest strategy to preserve some semblance of a separate identity. With this understanding of himself and with a painful awareness of how much he longed then and longs now for someone to love him with respect, he was in a position to look carefully at his life to see how he runs from the possibility of similar disappointment in current relationships. The first act of changing his current relational style had to be to open himself to feeling the pain of his past. Only then would he be in a position to realize how deeply determined he was to never feel that pain again. Only then could his strategies of self-protection in the present be exposed in all their ugliness. His style of relating (either academic or angry but rarely warm) could be recognized as a means to keeping himself at arm's length from others.

Many elements combine to promote real change. But moving on to deeper levels of involvement with others required this man to more deeply feel his pain and to face his self-protective sin. The more deeply we enter our disappointment, the more thoroughly we can face our sin. Unless we feel the pain of being victimized, we will tend to limit the definition of our problem with sin to visible acts of transgression.

Feeling disappointment has another advantage. It frees us to genuinely appreciate our parents, spouses, children, and friends for all the kindness they've extended to us and the qualities they display. Some of us have been blessed with wonderful parents who cared deeply for us and gave sacrificially to promote our happiness.

As a parent of older children (our two boys are now nineteen and seventeen), I am aware of having failed them, sometimes badly. But I also think I've done much that is good. A realistic assessment would grant me some rather high grades—always corrupted by imperfect love, but high nonetheless. My wife, too, is an excellent mother and truly deserves their gratitude. Do I really want my children to read this book? Would I be pleased if they looked closely at the ways in which I've failed them? The answer is a clear yes, *provided they faced their disappointment in order to love more deeply.*

Deficient love is always central to our problems. When someone appreciates his parents only because he overlooks the pain they caused him, his appreciation is not only superficial, it is really self-protective. Love is never blind to others' faults. It sees them clearly, but is not threatened. It admits disappointment, but forgives and continues to be warmly involved. Is there a tender concern for the welfare of one who treats you wrongly? That is the measure of love.

When we look clearly at how another has failed us, it can free us of our demand that they love us well. An obsessively high estimate of our parents' love for us often reflects our need to be loved rather than a realistic appraisal of their involvement. Demanding nothing of our parents allows us to appreciate whatever they do give. We must not ask more of our parents (or anyone else) than they can provide. Resentment toward parents (or spouses, children, friends) grows out of a demanding dependency that they satisfy us well. There is a difference between an angry, complaining look at another's failure and an honest admission of the disappointment their behavior provoked. The latter can dispel resentment; the former strengthens it.

Every non-organically caused problem has its deepest root in compromised love. Psychological difficulties and emotional problems are properly called "functional disorders" because they have a function. Anorexia provides women who've been stripped of any legitimate sense of personal identity and impact with a means of controlling both internal urges and other people's emotions. They have been sinned against and they sin.

Depressed people have been disappointed by others and feel a terrible internal vacuum. Their response is to cling desperately to a particular goal or special person they believe will keep them intact. When they don't reach the goal or the special person lets them down, depression sets in. They have been sinned against and they sin.

Male homosexuals have very little confidence in their ability to give to a woman what a close relationship requires. Involvement with a man feels far more comfortable because they are not asked to provide in that relationship what they fear might not be theirs to give. Their doubts about maleness stem more from damaging influences than personal choice. But their movement toward opportunities for intimacy where they never have to face their doubts is an effort to deal with deep problems through their own means. It is digging a broken well. They have been sinned against and they sin.[1]

We have all been sinned against. We all sin. You have failed to love me as you should and I have failed to love you. Your failure to love me is painful, sometimes profoundly disappointing. But the Lord's love for me is perfect. Although His love does not remove the sting of your failure, it gives me all I need to stand as a whole person, capable of loving you regardless of the threat of your further failure.

And that is my responsibility: to love you. My love for you (not yours for me) determines in large measure my experience of joy and my sense of intactness. I can love because I am loved perfectly and fully by God. And my love for you matters. It can draw you to Christ; it gives my life power and value in His plan; it brings glory to God. And, as I falteringly learn to love you without self-protection, I edge toward the longed-for reality of abundant living.

The struggle to live in disappointing relationships will continue until heaven. But the good news of the gospel is that there's a solution to the real problem. The sin of self-protection can be dealt with now.

NOTES

1. These brief descriptions of several disorders are not intended to be comprehensive statements about the nature and causes of the problems. I offer them only to make the point that beneath every struggle there is disappointment and self-protection.

CHAPTER ELEVEN

THE POWER OF THE GOSPEL

Is it *really* possible to change? Can a woman molested as a child *really* learn to embrace her sexuality? Do men with homosexual urges ever *really* become heterosexual? Can people who worry too much about money or their kids, or a couple whose marriage is no more exciting than a television rerun, or people with bad tempers *really* change?

The word "really" is the issue. In many people's minds, change must be nearly complete—at least dramatic—or it doesn't count. And the change required to convince us we've found the secret of growth must be the change we want the most: perhaps a new set of feelings including a warm desire to love and a peaceful strength as we handle life's problems or a deep desire to do right in the midst of temptation or a passionate appreciation of the Lord that eliminates any feelings of despair or battles against resentment.

If efforts to restore a drab marriage lead only to a flicker of warmth, then perhaps it hasn't really changed. If a homosexual man, after years of faithful commitment to his wife, reports a growing desire for relationship with her but admits he still struggles with homosexual temptation, maybe he hasn't really changed. Isn't God's power sufficient to set that marriage ablaze with love and to change a homosexual into a fully developed heterosexual? Why settle for less when God is at work?

Evangelicals sometimes expect too much or, to put it more precisely, we look for a kind of change God hasn't promised. It's possible to expect too little, but under-expectation is usually a cynical reaction to dashed hopes for too much. We manage to interpret biblical teaching to support our longing for perfection. As a result, we measure our progress by standards we will never meet until heaven.

Paul prays we may be strengthened with "power through his Spirit in your inner being" and asserts that God is "able to do immeasurably more than all we ask or imagine" (Ephesians 3:16,20). We therefore claim God's power as the guarantee of total change from pressure to peace, from disappointment to joy—and then live with an intolerable burden that either crushes us with despair or requires us to pretend we're better than we are.

The idea that peace and joy might merely *support* us during times of struggle and sorrow rather than *eliminate* those times is not appealing. We want to do away with the necessary pain of living in a disappointing world as imperfect people. We insist on experiencing neither pain nor failure, so when the inevitable happens, it becomes reason for discouragement.

We will, of course, be flawless—one day. No hint of perverted desire, no sleepless nights when our mind races mercilessly from one worry to another, no fear of becoming close to people that's fueled by memories of earlier hurt. All that is ahead of us, in heaven. But for now, struggles continue. There is a necessary pain of living in this world that we must simply accept. *But there are unnecessary problems that develop when we insist that necessary pain be eliminated.* Change from the inside out helps us move toward a substantial reduction in the severity and number of these unnecessary problems as we deal with the demand that energizes our self-protective maneuvering.

If we look for ways to get rid of necessary pain, we'll be disillusioned or misled. For people who define real change as the elimination of inevitable struggle, the final chapters will be terribly disappointing.

Unnecessary Problems Versus Necessary Responses

Through personal experience, I'm aware that digging about in our life to find relational pain and self-protective sin is difficult business. And unlike the miner whose spade work is rewarded by the glistening of precious metal, it seems the more we dig, the more mud we uncover.

Parents who looked pretty good come to be seen, at least in some areas, as terribly disappointing.

The logical response to the mud we uncover seems to be to cover it up again or to find some way to rinse it clean. To stand there, making no effort to move away from the pain, seems utterly unreasonable. When Adam was caught with his pants down, so to speak, his first thought was to find a tree to hide behind or to sew leaves into a covering. Standing still in our world, guilty and disappointed (Eve had not been an effective helper), is perhaps the hardest thing for us to do. To make no effort to clean up the mess and to live without self-protection is terrifying. It makes no sense. It feels like the route to death.

We might be persuaded to dig about in our life, in spite of the personal chaos it creates, if we could do something about the pain we uncover. If peace without pressure was guaranteed, if a joy that put an end to internal aching was available soon, then the cost of an inside look might be worth it. But if change from the inside out does nothing to relieve the necessary pain in our soul, then no matter what other desirable benefits might come, the price seems too high.

If we were convinced that the trauma of learning to trust God would *really* change us, we might be willing to endure it. But real change is available now; it's just not the kind of change we want. We insist that the real change heaven will bring (an end to all pain) be ours today. *That insistence is the problem we must overcome if the real change that's possible now is to occur.*

Perhaps a simple sketch shown on the following page will make the matter clear.

The dirt on the inside of the cup and dish is our demand for the relief of necessary pain, a demand that leads to self-protective

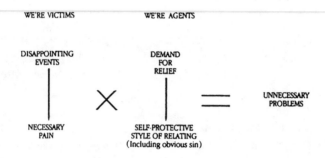

relational patterns designed to protect us from a disappointing world. As this dirt is cleaned up, unnecessary problems subside. It's necessary that we hurt, *but it's not necessary that we become less loving and less powerful people.* Chronic grumpiness, self-absorbing depression, anxiety over problems that keeps our attention riveted on what must be avoided, bad images of ourselves that interfere with giving ourself confidently and warmly to our family and friends: these are *unnecessary problems* that rob us of both the meaningful power to influence others for good and the penetrating love that encourages others to pursue the Lord.

There is a big difference between these unnecessary problems and a *necessary response to the problems in our world.* We cannot avoid necessary pain and struggle. We inevitably experience internal pressure that requires us either to collapse angrily or to press on in faith, feelings of discouragement that threaten to undo us, heartbreak over loved ones who reject us, despair that collapses us into dependence on God. These responses can be numbed only if we happen to live in a world that provides enough pleasant events to support the pretense that things are really quite good. But the soul that's aware will hurt.

The present power of the gospel lies *not* in its ability to generate an internal warmth that overcomes every experience of disappointment and struggle. If that's its claim, then I'm ashamed of the gospel. But if its claim is that dead people can live, that people who haven't the slightest hope of eternal happiness can live in Paradise forever, that a way has been made for sinners who deserve to suffer at the hands of a wrathful God to be declared righteous and therefore fit for relationship with God, then, with Paul, I am not ashamed. Any effort to lay out the path to a changed life now must be viewed in the context of these larger issues. Otherwise, we will ask too much and might fail to see that our core problem is an expectation for what cannot be that turns into a demand for relief from necessary pain.

The gospel's power today lies in its resources to help us overcome a demanding spirit and to replace it with trust as we await the full revelation of its power, the day when sinful people will enter heaven as loving worshipers of God, when further sin will be unthinkable and pain will be unknown.

We do have resources for dealing with disappointing events, necessary pain, and obvious sin, and we should use them. Although these resources don't solve our core problem, they can be an important part of the change process. Let me consider them briefly before talking about the central route to inside-out change.

Dealing with Disappointing Events
(Problems in Our World)

"What can I do to help my children become more responsible?" "How can I develop better friends?" "What should I do to help my wife? She seems so discouraged."

When we face troubling circumstances, we need to think carefully about the way we respond. Our desires for mature children, close friends, and encouraged mates are legitimate; I earlier called them critical longings. And the primary resources for handling problems in our world are *prayer* and biblical *principles*.

"Lord, work in my daughter's life. As I seek to love and lead her, create in her a desire to live for You." It's right to pray for matters that deeply concern us. And we should ponder those biblical passages that provide instruction for responding to the difficulties we face, whether irresponsible kids, overbearing employers, totalitarian governments, discouraged wives, ailing bodies, or insufficient funds.

Dealing with Necessary Pain (Pain in Our Heart)

When praying and applying biblical principles do not manage to correct the difficult situation, we are left to deal with the distress it creates. The focus then shifts from *changing our world* to *soothing our pain*.

This focus seems to be our contemporary preoccupation. No one but an idealistic adolescent, freshly scrubbed by Bible college and eager to live for God, thinks life will always go well. Because something really is wrong with everything and because the evidence of that dismal truth smacks us from time to time with a bitter sting, realism requires us to be concerned not only with hoping for better times but also with dressing our wounds.

We've developed the idea that the comfort of God can be applied to our wounds as an ointment that immediately relieves pain while it slowly promotes healing. However, the rhetoric about God's presence, especially in our hymnbooks, speaks about more than most of us experience. Reminders of God's love and exhortations to meditate on Jesus' care sometimes provide about as much help as handing out recipes to people waiting in a food line. They want *food*, not descriptions of it.

In recent years, a great deal of attention has been given to developing methods for finding comfort in God's truth. The intent of these methods, such things as guided meditation or memory healing, is to directly relieve hurt by focusing deeply on comforting but neglected realities.

These techniques have been severely criticized as blending too well with New Age ideas about inner voices and the like,[1] but their emphasis on meditation with the help of images that reflect biblical truth is legitimate. The Scriptures are filled with imagery designed to vividly highlight truths in a way bare statement does not. It's good to picture the still waters and green pastures with our Shepherd's commending presence shutting out all disruption. It's appropriate to find comfort in the realization that the hairs on our head have been counted. But it doesn't go far enough. It's possible to fix our attention on wonderful things about God in order to ignore terrible things about ourselves. Molested women who visualize Jesus deeply and respectfully caring about them, even during those moments when they were horribly violated, may use that visualization to avoid facing images of themselves that still guide their interactions.[2]

There are some problems we must *enter* rather than *numb*. Change from the inside out involves a steadfast gaze upon our Lord that's life changing because it reflects a deep turning from a commitment to self-sufficiency. Without repentance, a look at Christ provides only the illusion of comfort.

Dealing with Obvious Sin (Sin in Our Behavior)

In earlier chapters, I have already commented on the inadequacy of trying to promote change by focusing only on obvious sin. The struggle to endure pain and run the race without getting tangled up in sin is real work. Moral discipline is required. We must resist temptations to read pornography or to yell at our kids. We must strengthen ourself by spending time in God's Word.

But more is involved. The grime has been so imbedded in the carpet that a simple vacuuming will not do the job. We need a scrub brush and strong detergent. Working diligently to straighten up our actions without understanding either what it means to deeply repent or what it is that needs to be scrubbed away by repentance will make us more smug than penetrating. We'll pressure others to do right rather than draw them to want to do right.

We must do better than that. Change from the inside out requires more than:

> ➢ dealing with *problems in our world* by praying and trying to respond biblically;
> ➢ handling *pain in our heart* by reflecting on comforting truth; and
> ➢ responding to *sin in our behavior* by determining to resist temptation.

We must find some way to work on the *sin in our heart* that demanding spirit, that commitment to finding the happiness now

that only heaven will bring, that style of relating designed to protect us from the awful truth that we don't have what we so desperately want. The rest of this book will focus on what it means
to *repent* of sin in the heart.

Dealing with Relational Sin (Sin in the Heart)

I am convinced that most Christians simply do not think about
this category of sin. Certainly we understand it's wrong to be
unkind or malicious or backbiting, and we can easily accept the
idea that God is not pleased when we violate love. But entering
into the deep pain of our souls in order to see how subtly but stubbornly we keep our distance from one another in an effort to protect ourselves from that pain is an approach to understanding
relational sin that is not widely considered.

Highly trained theologians, zealously compassionate pastors,
strongly committed businessmen, remarkably talented women can
all continue for years in their Christian life without seriously
examining the sinfulness in their style of relating. It's possible to be
competent in theology and, at the same time, blind to the central
message of Christianity: we've been called into relationship with
God so we may relate more deeply with others. I don't see how
substantial progress in relating as we should is possible without
understanding and dealing with the relational sin of self-protection.

Change is a lifelong process of facing how alone we feel in all
of our relationships, how badly we want what even the best marriage or friendship can't provide, and then going on to see how
stubbornly committed we are to not feeling the necessary ache of
profound disappointment. Until we recognize with tears how determined we are to move away from pain and how that determination reflects our blasphemous decision to preserve our own life,
we will not be able to identify the subtle ways in which our relational style violates love for others by keeping us safe.

When openness to Scripture, to the whispering of God's Spirit,
and to the honest feedback of fellow Christians leads to an awareness of relational sin, then, and only then, is deep repentance possible. Repentance requires far more than a recognition that we're

sinful and sometimes sin. It requires an awareness of sin in its ugliest form, one that leads us in self-disgust to radically shift our direction from self-protection to love. It requires that we spot some of the specific ways we protect ourselves as we communicate with our mate, interact at a committee meeting, or socialize after church, and that we change those ways of relating because we want to move toward others regardless of personal risk.

Once we understand the concept of relational sin, we repent by *radically shifting our motivation and direction from self-preservation to trust on the basis of the belief that Christ has given and is preserving our life.* The fruit of repentance is a changed style of relating that replaces self-protective maneuvering with loving involvement.

In an arresting passage in Hosea 14:1-3, God tells the Jews of Hosea's day exactly how to repent. The passage points out the essentials of repentance that is real and deep.

> Return, O Israel, to the LORD your God. Your sins have been your downfall! Take words with you and return to the LORD. Say to him: "Forgive all our sins and receive us graciously, that we may offer the fruit of our lips. Assyria cannot save us; we will not mount war-horses. We will never again say 'Our gods' to what our own hands have made, for in you the fatherless find compassion."

Consider the elements of true repentance highlighted in this passage.

"Return to the LORD your God"

The key to all change is returning to God. Christ defined eternal life as knowing God (John 17:3), and by His atoning death made it possible for sinful people to be restored to relationship with God. Growth in the Christian life means coming to know God better. *Every effort to change must involve at its core a shift in direction away from dependence on one's own resources for life to dependence on God.*

It's possible to deal with problems in our world by praying and doing our best to obey biblical principles, to look for relief from the pain in our heart through contemplating marvelous truths, to responsibly obey God by resisting the temptation to sin in our behavior, and still continue moving away from God by relating to others through self-protective walls. The Christian's call is to relationship, to loving, non-defensive involvement with others.

"Take words with you"

Repentance is more than a general commitment to change. The implication of God's requirement to take words with us as we approach Him in repentance is that we must have some clear idea of what we're repenting of. The more thorough our awareness of sin, the more complete our repentance. Because we'll never see ourself exactly as we are until heaven, the prayer that God cleanse us from secret faults is always appropriate. But it must never be used as an excuse for not exploring our problem with sin.

"Forgive all our sins"

Repentance is a turning away from sin that's made possible by God's willingness to forgive us. Unnecessary problems can sometimes be relieved by changing circumstances, soothing heartache, and doing right things, but such change will not lead to a realization of our potential to powerfully love people. We will genuinely love only as we deal with the sin in our heart.

"Receive us graciously, that we may offer the fruit of our lips"

So many of our efforts to change have a hidden but definite agenda. The motivation to work on our life is usually sustained by the hope that difficult circumstances will improve and painful feelings will go away. "Okay, I'll go for counseling. Maybe that will wake him up." Or "I must spend more time with the Lord; I've been feeling so depressed lately."

True repentance, on the other hand, is energized by the hope of knowing and worshipping God more richly. "Receive us so we may worship" is the thought of the text. But for so many Christians, the word worship means little more than spending an hour every Sunday morning quietly reflecting on God, listening to occasionally stirring messages about Him, and feeling inspired now and then by the music. We will be driven to true worship only as we give up on all earthly hopes of fending life (which requires that we face our disappointments in every relationship), and grow in our understanding that there is life in Christ and nowhere else.

"Assyria cannot save us; we will not mount war-horses"

Israel was threatened with national collapse. The country was weak and vulnerable. Like people who feel scared normally do, the people of Israel looked for help to resources that were immediately available: a pact with Assyria to protect them combined with their own military efforts might win the day.

If a mugger approached me, I'd run, scream for help, spray mace in his eyes, or give him my wallet to save my neck. But when the essential well-being of my soul is attacked, I must not protect myself, even though an effort to preserve myself from destruction seems like the right thing to do. To do so leads to death. Christ could not have contradicted natural wisdom more completely when He taught that life is found by making no effort to keep it.

Israel turned to Assyria and war-horses for her national survival. We resort to self-protective maneuvering in our patterns of relating to ensure personal survival. Repentance requires a sincere admission that whatever we're depending on for life will let us down. Assyria cannot save us. Self-protection is futile. We will therefore shift our direction away from depending on our own resources to vulnerably trusting God. If He fails to come through, then we'll be destroyed. That is the recognition that leads to change.

"We will never again say 'Our gods' to what our own hands have made"

This is the core of repentance. Thirsty people are invited to come to Christ. But because we're not only thirsty but also foolishly rebellious, we grab our shovels and run into the wilderness (or into Canaan) to dig our own water supply. We're determined, with all the intensity of someone struggling to survive, to maintain control over our own welfare. Trust does not come easily to fallen people.

But it must come. And its development requires a clear and decisive break with self-sufficiency. Our attempts to preserve a sense of competence and personal security as we relate to others must be identified and forsaken. The efficiently hard woman who has been let down by a weak father and a weaker husband must see that her crisp style of relating functions as her protection against further pain. She must decide to give up that crispness and choose the tough road of vulnerable sharing and risky involvement. Doing so will seem like suicide, but it is the path to life. "Whoever loses his life for me will save it" (Luke 9:24).

"In you the fatherless find compassion"

Fatherless children are unprotected, vulnerable to the point of helplessness. Repentance leads us into an experience of our disappointment and aloneness that crushes us with a pain that cannot be relieved. But when we trust God in our helplessness enough to move toward other people simply because that is God's will for us, then the reality of His compassion slowly begins to enter our soul. As we walk a path that seems to lead toward death, a sense of life quietly grows within us.

The Fruits of Repentance

When repentance moves us from self-protection to obedient trust, then God moves in changing power. He heals our waywardness (Hosea 14:4) so our compulsive desire to sin no longer masters us. He deepens our roots (verse 5), creating a new stability. He grants us splendor and an appealing fragrance (verse 6); our life becomes attractive. People dwell in our shade (verse 7), suggesting that others are blessed by our strength. We learn that our fruitfulness comes from God (verse 8), and our heart worships Him with gratitude and love.

"Who is wise? He will realize these things. Who is discerning? He will understand them. The ways of the LORD are right; the righteous walk in them, but the rebellious stumble in them" (Hosea 14:9).

Repentance that follows this model leads to a change in our character. Problems in our world remain. We still hurt. We sometimes do wrong things. But the more clearly we recognize how our deep commitment to self-protection operates in our relational style and the more courageously we face the ugliness of protecting ourself rather than loving others, the more we'll shift our direction. Repentance, a deep change of mind about the source of life that admits there is life in Christ and nothing else, produces an increasing strength, stability, and attractiveness that represents change from the inside out.

Repentance is neither a complete cure nor an easy one. The price is high. For repentance to be deep enough to wash away substantial amounts of our inside dirt, we must endure some hard times. The next chapter describes the route to deep repentance.

NOTES

1. Sometimes the criticism is entirely justified. New Age thinking and Christianity do not complement one another. In all their essential teaching, they blatantly contradict. Integration opens the door to influence from false spirits. That, of course, must be avoided.

2. Abused women often see themselves as cheap and dirty, utterly alone in those parts of their soul where they most desperately long for involvement. Images of Christ designed to soothe their pain can provide the means of never entering their pain and therefore failing to come to grips with their commitment to self-protection. Such techniques can thus obscure the necessity for repentance.

CHAPTER TWELVE

WHAT IT TAKES TO DEEPLY CHANGE

Perhaps the most confusing question that emerges from a study of change from the inside out is this: *How far inside do you have to look?* Once we agree an inside look is necessary for deep change, we enter the mouth of a dark cave that tunnels off in endless, uncharted directions.

There will always be more to see: buried emotions that never disturbed us until we surfaced them, devious purposes that didn't seem to interfere with reasonably effective living until we exposed them, painful feelings of sadness that can turn the brightest morning into a long gloomy day. We could spend a lifetime exploring the winding caverns of our soul and never come out into sunlight.

Although an inside look can be overwhelming (and indeed must be if the core direction of our life is to really shift), still there must be more to it than a journey into darkness. We are children of light. Even in the midst of darkness, we know where we're headed. We have a lamp that always reveals the next step and a hope that keeps us moving even when the lamp seems to go out. Christians are not to be characterized by joyless confusion and morbid despair. And that's precisely what develops when we define the path to growth as an endless search for further awareness of all that's happening within us.

We must not mistake an intense, absorbing heaviness for spiritual depth. Spiritual depth frees us to be spontaneous in the midst of sadness. It enables us to press on in our involvement with people even when we stagger from blows of severe disappointment. A mature relationship with Christ is reflected in the capacity to hear whispers of assurance when discouragement is oppressive. And even when we're mishandling frustration by retreating into an angry pout, mature depth won't let us escape the convicting awareness that we're designed to love, even in *this* situation.

The purpose of an inside look is to promote that kind of spiritual depth. The more deeply we sense our thirst, the more passionately we'll pursue water. And the more clearly we recognize how we dig our own wells in search of water, the more fully we can repent of our self-sufficiency and turn to God in obedient trust. As we learn to live in confidence that the deepest concerns of our soul are in good hands, both the shame we feel because of our unworthiness and the terror we have of one day facing exposure and rejection will lose their power to control us. Change from the inside out involves a gradual shift away from self-protective relating to strongly loving involvement. And in order to make that change, we must feel our disappointment as a longing person and face the sin in our heart that results in a commitment to self-protection.

But how far should we go with this? Are we to spend hours, maybe years, pondering how badly we've been sinned against until we run out of painful memories? Must we look for new insights about ourself in every dream, every slip of the tongue, every emotion? Should we scrutinize every word we say to see if perhaps a speck of self-protection remains? This business of an inside look could become ridiculous—and damaging. Yet an inside look is necessary. Risky, but necessary if we are to move beyond superficial change to change from the inside out. What must we understand about ourself and about God in order to change? What must an inside look reveal if change is to occur at the deepest level?

Change in the Christian life is progressive. We move from change in our conscious direction to *change in our approach to relationships* to *change in the direction of our very being.* Each change represents a work of God and is therefore good. To label the first kind of change shallow would wrongly demean it. But to stop with the first kind of change, or the second, rejects a failure to understand the opportunity we have to pursue God and to know Him. New believers change in their conscious direction. Growing believers learn to love by abandoning their self-protection. Mature believers begin to grasp the meaning of Paul's words, "For to me, to live is Christ," as they shift the central direction of their very being toward God. What does an inside look contribute to the progress from one level of growth to the next? What does it take to deeply change?

Change in Our Conscious Direction

I teach at a seminary. I have the opportunity to see dozens of young people whose lives have been changed by God. One young man comes to mind who recently shared his testimony with several students and faculty. He told of his days "in the world" when his life revolved around rock music, girls, and fun. Through a marvelous set of circumstances that were clearly ordered by God, this young rock musician was converted to Christ. He immediately changed his lifestyle.

The rock band in which he played was about to move from engagements in local bars to "big-time" clubs. The promise of money and fame was appealing, but he quit. He decided God wanted him in the ministry and therefore he reenroll in college, this time a Christian one, with plans to go on to seminary. As he told his story, it was clear he was excited about the change in direction God had brought about in his life. And properly so. We all rejoiced with him because of his conversion and his dedication to the Lord.

From a hard rock band to a seminary classroom: that's change. But it's a change that leaves important areas in his soul untouched. Although he's made a radical shift in direction, there's more within him that must be changed. What's taken place represents a wonderful work of God, but it's only the beginning in the entire redirecting of a human life.

Change in Our Approach to Relationships

The situation with this changed student is roughly parallel to an adulterer who repents of his sin and returns to his wife. His movement away from immorality and back to faithful husbanding is good. But now he must confront the things within himself and his marriage that spoiled his earlier efforts to love her. His work is just beginning.

A change in one's conscious direction requires an awareness of only a few basic truths that must be embraced and obeyed. Both the seminary student and the repentant husband understood they had sinned, that the wages of sin is death, that the gift of life from God can only be gratefully received and never earned, that Christians are bought with a price, that sin is an offense against our Father that He will not take lightly, and that we're called to live holy lives of service for Him.

For anyone to believe all these truths is itself a miracle of God's grace. In our efforts to "go deeper," we must not sell it short. But neither should we settle into a complacent orthodoxy that stunts further growth. There's more to learn about sin and God and directing our life toward Him. If we don't press on toward more, the good we have will sour like unused milk. If that eager seminarian lives the next thirty years without taking an inside look, the hard shell of self-protection will encase his heart, and his life will eventually have the impact of a clanging cymbal. Like so many other seasoned veterans, he will faithfully expound truth but will penetrate very few lives.

To become effective in our interactions with people, we must change in our approach to relationships. We must turn from self-protective maneuvering to a rich involvement that deeply touches people. And that turn occurs only through repentance. To meaningfully repent of the ways in which we violate love, we must recognize them. We won't recognize self-protective patterns of relating as sinful violations of love until we face the disappointment in our soul we're determined to never experience again.

As the young preacher, now graduated from seminary, prepares his sermons, visits members of his congregation, and does what he can to keep the church unified and active, he may never take the time to reflect on the deep ache in his soul that comes from living in a fallen world. When the ache creeps into aware-ness, perhaps provoked by a contentious elder who's undermining his work, the pastor's commitment to keep his distance from over-whelming pain may corrupt his response to the elder. He may sim-ply refuse to deal with the man; he may compromise what he believes in order to keep the peace; he may adopt his most intim-idating posture and confront him. And the demanding spirit, the self-preserving purpose of whatever strategy he selects, may go entirely unrecognized.

Without an awareness of internal disappointment and pain that makes him yearn for relief and without an understanding of the subtle ways in which he honors his determination to find that relief, the pastor may adopt a style of relating that can harden into the distance of cold orthodoxy or weaken into gentle but power-less accommodation. Either way, the man who changed his direc-tion from playing rock music to preaching the Word may develop an approach to relationships that's utterly devoid of gripping vital-ity. To become a person with power in relationships, he must take an inside look.

When we make a commitment to integrity and openness, an inside look will expose previously hidden disappointments that provoke a frightening level of rage at those who hurt us. When we admit the pain of disappointment and the rage of betrayal, we can then see how our style of relating has been shaped by a stubborn commitment to avoid feeling the pain and, in many cases, expressing the rage. At the point where we recognize self-protective relational patterns as a defense against pain, an inside look has done important work. It has made possible a deeper level of repentance. Until we reach that point, repentance is little more than an admission of wrongdoing followed by concerted effort to do better. When we fully understand our disappointed thirst and self-protective patterns, repentance can involve a deeper shift in our understanding of *how life is to be lived* and *how we miss the* mark. Unless an inside look genuinely uncovers these two elements, we will change neither our conscious direction nor our approach to relationships.

222 CHANGING FROM THE INSIDE OUT

Suppose our seminary student becomes aware of feeling nervous as he completes his theological training and accepts a church position. He notices that the nervousness is sometimes displaced by an almost cocky confidence. Rather than burying these confusing emotions beneath stronger commitments to ministry and more time spent in the Word, he properly regards his feelings as flashing lights on the dashboard of his car telling him to pull over and look beneath the hood. With an awareness of his dignity as an image-bearer who was built for God as well as his depravity as a rebel who wants to independently manage his own life, he looks inside for evidence of both disappointed thirst and determination to provide for his own relief.

As he ponders the idea of having been sinned against, he remembers painful incidents with his father. "Can't you do anything right?" his dad yelled when he scraped the fender of the new family car. The intense feelings he has as he recalls that incident suggest his father's angry words penetrated deeply into important parts of his soul. He begins to understand that he feels a chronic sense of inadequacy that runs beneath most of his life.

As he thinks back to times when his self-esteem was threatened and recalls how he handled himself, a pattern becomes clear. His typical response to troubling encounters has been to display his upset, hoping the offending person would be shamed into providing support. With this insight, he is able to repent more meaningfully. When he feels nervous, he can accurately identify his fear of doing something wrong that might cost him the respect and approval of others. And, more important, he can recognize his inclination to manipulate people into supporting him.

As he discusses these thoughts with his wife, perhaps she'll be able to find the courage to tell him how much she dreads the ride home from church every Sunday. His insistence that she report any comments or criticisms she heard about his sermon makes her uncomfortable. She's beginning to see him as a weak man, and she's gradually losing respect for him.

Equipped with a basic understanding of the pain in his heart and the form his demand for relief often assumes, the pastor recognizes his need to trust God more deeply and to repent of his self-protection. The next Sunday, as they drive home from church, he puts his hand on his wife's knee and says, "I'm dying to hear how I did this morning, but I really don't need to know. Let me take you out to dinner with an agreement to not even mention church."

This, I suggest, represents a change in his approach to relationships. An inside look at his thirst and self-protection made it possible. In thirty years, if he continues to grow by repenting of self-protection whenever he sees it and entrusting the care of his threatened soul to Christ, he'll be more than a clanging cymbal. He'll be a struggling but strong and loving man who's been used by God to deeply touch many lives.

Change in the Direction of Our Being

Repenting of relational strategies designed to protect us from internal pain is wonderful. But there's still more potential for change from the inside out. Not only can we change in our conscious direction and shift from self-protective maneuvering to more loving involvement, but we can also change the direction of our very being from idolatry to worship. We can come to realize that pestering our wife for encouraging feedback is far more than a "wrong strategy designed to protect us from pain." The clinical feel of that assessment can be replaced with a gripping awareness of the idolatrous roots of the maneuver, an awareness that makes us pant after God with all our heart, soul, mind, and strength.

The redirection of our soul requires far more than cosmetic surgery or even a major operation. To move on toward an increasing maturity that yields the life-changing power of deep love requires a further look inside. Before I suggest what more must be uncovered, let me sketch (see the next page) what I've said so far.

The question posed at the beginning of this chapter must now be answered: *What must an inside look uncover before deep change is possible?* A basic grasp of the gospel can change our conscious direction. If we're to change our approach to relationships we must know what it means to be let down and see how we protect ourself from further disappointment. But what does the Bible tell us about changing the direction of our very being?

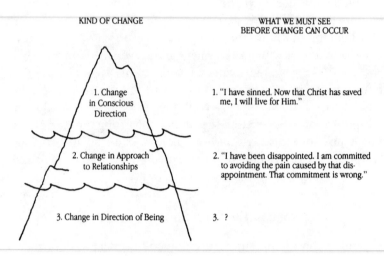

KIND OF CHANGE	WHAT WE MUST SEE BEFORE CHANGE CAN OCCUR
1. Change in Conscious Direction	1. "I have sinned. Now that Christ has saved me, I will live for Him."
2. Change in Approach to Relationships	2. "I have been disappointed. I am committed to avoiding the pain caused by that disappointment. That commitment is wrong."
3. Change in Direction of Being	3. ?

The most profound level of change possible before heaven requires an inside look at two hard-to-grasp realities: (1) since the Fall, every man struggles to regard himself as fully male and every woman struggles to regard herself as fully female; and (2) life between the fall of man and the coming of Christ is so overwhelmingly sad that only our hope in Christ can preserve us from insanity or suicide.

Neither our struggle with sexual identity nor the sadness of life is a matter that lends itself to simple explanation. Either topic could easily justify a book-length discussion. I include some basic thoughts about them only because I believe there's a depth of change that cannot be realized apart from facing the issues raised by these concerns.

1. We See Ourselves as Weakened Men and Damaged Women.

When God created human beings, He made us male and female. No one is merely a person. We are either male persons or female persons, boys or girls, men or women. The uniqueness of being male or female reaches to the very core of our identity. Far more is involved in the distinction than clothing, hairstyle, voice pitch, or even anatomy. Everything a man does, he does as a man. Everything a woman does, she does as a woman.

When we're properly related to God and functioning according to His design, we live with a rich enjoyment of our sexual identity. Fully giving what I have to give as a man brings a deep sense of rightness. Something good is going on, like using just the right tool for a difficult job. Similarly, a woman who is free to be fully feminine in her relating feels an internal calm that comes from living consistently with who she is designed to be.

Men were designed to enter their worlds strongly, providing for their families, leading them (through servanthood) toward God, moving toward others with sacrificing, powerful love. Women were designed to courageously give all they have (intellect, talents, wisdom, kindness, and so on) to others in warm vulnerability, allowing themselves to be entered and wrapping themselves with supportive strength around those with whom they relate, offering all they are as female image-bearers for a godly purpose.

But something has gone wrong with the plan. When Paul sets out to demonstrate our need for the gospel, he describes people as so determined to live according to their own design that God has given them over to themselves (Romans 1:24,26,28). Three times, he reports, God gave them over to the inevitable consequences of insisting that they figure out life on their own.

The first "giving over" was to sexual desires, an important fact to notice. When Adam and Eve fell into sin, they lost relationship with God and, because of that separation, they also lost the opportunity to fully enjoy all they were as male and female. For Adam, working now meant a battle with weeds and thorns, a battle he wasn't able to fully overcome. He became threatened *as a man*, as a person designed to productively enter his world on behalf of another.

Eve could no longer count on Adam to respond to her with love. The support and vulnerability through which she'd expressed her womanliness now endangered her. She had to become tough and hard in order to handle the reality that Adam was no longer a perfect partner. She became threatened *as a woman*, as a person who finds joy in accepting and embracing others but who now feels compelled to defensively control her relationships.

With the loss of joyful freedom to fully express all we are as men and women, we sense a deep uneasiness, a restlessness that drives us to recapture the wholeness that comes from enjoying our sexual identity. But without God, the nearest we can come to rich and exciting enjoyment of that identity is fulfillment of our physical desires. Sexual excitement and climax provides fallen people with the closest available approximation to what it means to be fully alive as sexual beings. What was intended as the *expression* of our sexuality has become the *evidence*, even the *substance*, of it. Something vital to life as a human being has been lost. We no longer begin with a quiet confidence in our intactness as men who strongly enter and women who strongly accept.

We're not certain our masculine and feminine souls have the resources to remain alive no matter what failure or rejection comes our way; a sense of *substance* as men and women is simply no longer there. We feel driven to recover it. And because we're desperate to regain what we know should be there but isn't, we feel irresistibly drawn to sexual pleasures.

The experience of physical excitement and fulfillment gives us a few happy moments that make us feel alive as men and women. Sexual pleasures are compulsively attractive precisely because we no longer see ourselves as truly male and truly female. And when we doubt our essential identity as man or woman, we struggle. We do something about the problem, just as a pilot must take action when his engines stop running. An airplane without working engines cannot fly. And a person without an awareness of masculine or feminine intactness lodged deeply in his or her soul cannot live according to God's design.

The *problem* is threatened sexuality, an inevitable consequence of moving away from God. The *symptom* of the problem is sinful sexual expression. The *function* of the symptom is to provide a counterfeit, momentary sense of maleness or femaleness. And that, too, is sinful.

When people turn from God, the first thing they pursue when God removes His restraining hand is sexual pleasure. Soon they reflect their damaged identity by perverting their sexual desires in homosexual relations (Romans 1:26). Then, springing from the root of threatened identity as men and women, people engage in all kinds of sinful practices that corrupt their relational style (Romans 1:29-32).

I wonder if the energy with which we pursue sin grows out of the threat the Fall introduced to our identity as male and female. If that's true, and I think it is, then an inside look that gets to the bottom of things will expose our doubts about our ability to function as men and women. Until we sense the deep discomfort we feel in relating as men and women, we haven't touched the core of our struggle.

The primitive threat that's always present in fallen people (a legacy left to us by our first parents) makes boys aware of their weakness, incompetence, and helplessness. As they sense an impotence to enter their world with strength, they learn to compensate by emphasizing whatever special abilities or talents they discover in themselves. Or they generate a counterfeit sense of masculinity through aggression, rebellion, and exaggerated independence. Or they retreat into a passivity that wimpishly demands that someone take care of them.

Girls quickly feel violated and unsafe. Even the most caring parent will occasionally fail to come through with an appropriately loving response. Little girls learn their survival depends on tucking away that wonderful part of themselves that was designed to give vulnerably. When someone wins a girl's trust to the point where she risks exposing that deeply feminine desire to be entered, and then betrays her trust (sexual abuse is the worst form of betrayal), she comes to regard those desires within her as reason for shame and self-disgust.

At the very center of our soul, we feel shame and fear that is attached to our identity as male or female. Males lack the healthy confidence that they're intact men who can move into their world unafraid of being completely destroyed by failure or disrespect. Females lack that quietly exhilarating awareness that they're secure women who can embrace their world with no worry of having their essential identity crushed by someone's abuse or rejection.

Men pursue defensive strategies for living designed to compensate for their lack of confidence. Some dominate their families and call it spiritual leadership. Others neglect their families and friends in favor of the opportunity to make money, to become manager, or to build their church. The energy behind these self-protective maneuvers is tied to their threatened identity as men.

Women exaggerate their physical appeal or hide it behind a stiff competence. Some become docile children who accept the demeaning control of someone who will take care of them. Their defensive style of relating is geared primarily to protect themselves from facing the threat they feel as women.

The feelings of shame so deeply attached to our doubts about our maleness or femaleness provide powerful motivation to protect ourselves from further wounds. *We will not face our self-protective maneuvering nor be passionately convicted about its sinfulness until we see its function is to preserve whatever is left of our identity as men and women.*

When the happy-go-lucky husband realizes his refusal to sincerely communicate with his wife about difficult matters reflects a terrible fear that he may not have what it takes to win respect from her, then he can begin to face not only the terror of threatened manhood but also the thrill of its potential.

When the businesslike woman sees her fear of being exploited or disdained if she offers what's really inside her feminine heart, then she can better understand that her self-protection is a desperate attempt to hide her damaged womanhood. When she realizes that beneath her defensive hardness is a woman, wounded and afraid, she may get an exciting glimpse of what it would mean to be fully female, a glimpse that will both terrify and entice her.

Deep repentance includes giving up self-protection in order to more fully express the man or woman we were created to be. It liberates us to be the tender, strong, involved men and the secure, giving, vulnerable women who can live out God's design and more properly represent Him. Change at the deepest level requires a recognition that we see ourselves as weakened men and damaged women.

2. If We Honestly Face the Sadness of Life in a Fallen World, then Only Our Hope in Christ Can Preserve Us from Insanity or Suicide.

So much in our everyday living is designed to disguise the horror of living apart from God. Unbelievers often get along quite well.

Nominal Christians seem every bit as happy (often far more) than the deeply committed. It seems there is no real point in absolutely surrendering to God. Better to water down the concept of surrender and enjoy the satisfaction of being a "relatively good Christian." Decent people manage well. Fanatics get in trouble. The real key to life, we seem to think, is to keep things pleasant while we pursue God with a good bit of our heart, soul, mind, and strength.

This weakened version of Christianity can work if we refuse to face the overwhelming and unbearable sadness of life without God. But when we are able to maintain the fiction that life is tolerable at worst and quite satisfying at best, we sacrifice an appreciation for the two center points of our faith: the Cross of Christ and His Coming. The Cross becomes the means by which God delivers us from something not really too terrible, and the Coming is reduced to an opportunity for a merely improved quality of life. The Lord's Supper then becomes mere ritual. "Remember Me till I come" is an invitation that inspires little passion because the cross we're to remember is stripped of its awesome worth and the coming we're to anticipate becomes only a step up.

The joy we can know in this present world depends entirely on what the Lord Jesus Christ has done and what He yet will do. Remove the Cross and the Coming and every joy becomes an illusion, a deceptive illusion that keeps us from clinging to Christ with worshipful passion and eager anticipation.

Recently a student said to me, "I have felt some disappointment in every relationship I have, but I've only been bothered by it. It's never staggered me."

Most of us have never been staggered. Christians cooperate with nonChristians to preserve the appearance that things aren't really too bad, and in a sense, that's true. Marriages are sometimes rich; people can be extraordinarily kind and helpful; teenagers are often cooperative and reliable; jobs are sometimes meaningful and rewarding. But none of these good things about life can touch our soul with the satisfaction we desire. Until we grasp how deeply we long for what we do not have, our enjoyment of life's pleasures is defensive. We will depend on them to obscure the emptiness of our soul. To the degree we keenly feel the painful disappointment of unsatisfied longings, we're able to ask no more of life's pleasures than they're capable of providing. And then we can enjoy them realistically as legitimate tastes from the banquet table God will one day spread before us.

The illusion that life in a fallen world is really not too bad must be shattered. When even the best parts of life are exposed as pathetic counterfeits of how things should be, the reality drives us to a level of distress that threatens to utterly undo us. *But it's when we're on the brink of personal collapse that we're best able to shift the direction of our soul from self-protection to trusting love.* The more deeply we enter into the reality that life without God is sheer desolation, the more fully we can turn toward Him.

There is no place for sugarcoating in the life of a serious Christian. Life is unspeakably sad. But we're more than conquerors over every cause of sadness. Repentance means to accept the truth that life without God is no life at all and to therefore pursue God with all the passion of someone who has been rescued from unimaginable horror. When hints of sadness creep into our soul, we must not flee into happy or distracting thoughts. Pondering the sadness until it becomes overwhelming can lead us to a deep change in the direction of our being from self-preservation to grateful worship.

The richest love grows in the soil of an unbearable disappointment with life. When we realize life can't give us what we want, we can better give up our foolish demand that it do so and get on with the noble task of loving as we should. We will no longer need to demand protection from further disappointment. The deepest change will occur in the life of a bold realist who clings to God with a passion only his realistic appraisal of life can generate. Now we can complete the sketch as shown on the following page.

Let me conclude my discussion by telling the story of a friend of mine who is changing from the inside out. I tell it with his permission. Several details have been distorted to protect him from being identified by those who may know him; otherwise, the story is true in every important respect.

Tony trusted Christ at the end of his second year in college. He'd been raised in a tension-filled home that provided him little support or love. His parents apparently got along fairly well until

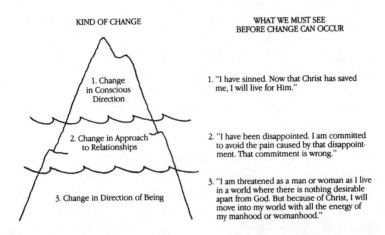

KIND OF CHANGE

WHAT WE MUST SEE
BEFORE CHANGE CAN OCCUR

1. Change in Conscious Direction

1. "I have sinned. Now that Christ has saved me, I will live for Him."

2. Change in Approach to Relationships

2. "I have been disappointed. I am committed to avoid the pain caused by that disappointment. That commitment is wrong."

3. Change in Direction of Being

3. "I am threatened as a man or woman as I live in a world where there is nothing desirable apart from God. But because of Christ, I will move into my world with all the energy of my manhood or womanhood."

Tony entered elementary school. From that time on, Tony remembers regular shouting matches between his parents, ended sometimes by his father leaving for a week or two and then begging to come back. He remembers his mother as a hard, controlling woman who never wept over her marriage but whose tears flowed freely whenever Tony retreated from her.

Until his conversion, Tony had lived for academic excellence. High grades provided the most reliable source of recognition he could find. He worked hard and stayed out of trouble. He expressed the deep bitterness he felt toward his parents, especially his domineering mother, by regularly breaking curfew and by maintaining a sullen, noncommunicative disposition.

When Tony came to Christ, there was definite change. He felt less antagonism toward his home life and made concerted efforts to treat his parents more kindly. Sensing a real desire to know more about the Bible and to serve God, he switched to a Christian college and soon decided he was called to enter some kind of full-time ministry.

After completing college with honors, he enrolled in an evangelical seminary. During his training there, he developed a burden for people that was evidenced by an increasingly sensitive and gentle spirit. The change in his personality softened his mother (his father died during his first year of seminary) to the point where she received Christ as Savior.

Tony had changed. God had done wonderful things both in him and through him. And the change in his conscious direction and general mood had not required a difficult look into painful and ugly parts of his soul. He knew he was a sinner, he understood the significance of Christ's death and resurrection, and he had a new purpose in life. That was enough.

When he completed his seminary program, he went to work for a Christian ministry that suited his interests and abilities. For nearly fourteen years, he continued in that ministry, earning a well-deserved reputation as a sincere, hardworking, committed Christian. He married a lovely woman and they had three children. Things were going well. His work was meaningful and satisfying. He loved his family, enjoyed good heath, and managed to afford a nice home and a relatively comfortable lifestyle.

Soon after he turned forty, a few problems appeared in Tony's life. A schoolteacher requested a conference with Tony and his wife to discuss their son, nearly eleven years old by this time. She reported that the boy seemed unmotivated, almost depressed, and had fallen seriously behind in his studies. When the teacher recommended referral to the school psychologist, Tony's wife panicked. Tony didn't know how to help his son or calm down his wife.

At the same time, one of Tony's colleagues, a long-time close friend, confided in Tony that he was terribly unhappy in his job and struggling with major family tensions no one suspected. Tony was stunned and dismayed, but did his best to encourage his friend. Over the next few weeks, Tony's friend pulled back from him and casually dismissed any effort on Tony's part to discuss his problems.

It was during that same time period that I had the opportunity to interact with Tony both in social settings and ministry projects. I didn't like the feeling, but I found myself hoping Tony wouldn't show up for committee meetings, and I definitely had little interest in more social time together. Tony always seemed to be up. No matter how bad things were, he consistently painted a positive picture. Difficult times were good, and good times were fantastic. I had a hard time enjoying his joy. It seemed to lack depth. Frankly, I felt bored when I was with Tony.

Three sources provided Tony with similar input within a relatively short period. The family counselor persuaded Tony's wife to admit that her panic over their son's problems was in part a fear that Tony simply wouldn't deal with how bad things were. Tony's good friend told him he'd felt very unsupported by Tony when he shared his problem. And during a long car ride, I took advantage of an opening to tell Tony his contribution to committee meetings seemed to skirt tough issues.

I deeply respect Tony. He's a man of integrity, willing to face whatever problems he might have. The three sources of input had made it clear to him that he wasn't dealing effectively with people in his world. He began to wonder why. As he spent time in prayer and in the Word and discussed his concern with others, he was looking inside to see what was keeping him from strong involvement with his wife, friend, and ministry.

The next few months were life-changing for Tony. He became aware of a frightened insistence that everything in his world be nice. As a youngster, he had known a few warm times—a summer with his grandparents, two weeks at a camp—but most of his memories were painful. He desperately wanted things to be pleasant. He wanted to feel secure in a comfortable world where everyone got along.

He learned to handle his disappointed longings by never facing up to how he really felt and by putting all his energy into whatever he did well. As it became clear to Tony that his relational style was to ignore tension and to warmly "require" that everyone be happy, he began to see the pressure he was putting on his son and wife and the way he failed to grapple honestly with problems in his relationships and ministry. When he could recognize the patterns as self-protective sin, he started to change. He repented of his determination to "trust Assyria" by keeping everything happy and looked for ways to enter more deeply into people's lives without demanding they give him warm feedback.

He opened up to his wife about some of his real hurts and learned to listen more carefully to hers. He talked honestly with his son about the issue of pressure. When his friend shared anything at all, he stopped himself from giving a helpful perspective and chose to listen first. At committee meetings, he let himself feel annoyed and dealt with it directly. He was significantly changing his relational style because of a new awareness of the patterns he used to protect himself from painful disappointment.

Some months later, Tony was sharing with a few close friends about the exciting changes taking place in his relationships with family members and others. When he finished, one man responded, "Tony, I really do think the change has been super and I praise God for it. I've seen it and felt it. But I'm confused. I'm not sure why, but I feel less excitement than I think I should as you report these great changes. I think your pattern of emphasizing the positive is still robbing you of real power and genuineness." The other friends agreed.

Lengthy discussion followed that focused on two issues. First, Tony began to face how emasculated he'd felt around a mother who dominated him and how powerless he'd felt to do anything about the terrible situation in his earlier family. He began to face his profound discomfort *as a man*.

Second, Tony faced another pattern. In the times when he pondered the imperfection of all his relationships, past and present, he would sometimes sense an overwhelming flood of sadness begin to rise in his soul. As soon as he felt the sadness coming, he would quickly stiffen his backbone and get on with doing whatever needed to be done. We encouraged him to reflect on the sadness of life and let it drive him to tears.

Two weeks after that discussion, I saw Tony. He walked up to me, put his hand solidly on my shoulder, and said, "I have a lot to think about. I really want to be a strong man for my family and friends. I've been reflecting on how hard I try to avoid any kind of suffering for fear I'm not man enough to handle it well. My time in Scripture has recently focused on the strength of Christ in my weakness and on the role of suffering in making me more like our Lord. I'm trembling a little, but I'm really looking forward to what God wants to do with me. It's exciting. I've never felt more alive."

As Tony talked, I wasn't bored. On the contrary, I was drawn to the God he was pursuing. With Tony, I was celebrating the kind of change that's possible when we're willing to start from the *inside out*.

CHAPTER THIRTEEN

THE "GOOD STUFF" BENEATH THE BAD

Change from the inside out requires that we take an unsettling look into ourselves that thoroughly disrupts our complacency. That look begins with an understanding of God's moral requirements and how far short we fall in our efforts to keep them.

It continues with a keen awareness of an inconsolable ache that nothing in time, nothing on earth, and nothing from another human being can fully relieve. Then it moves toward the brokenness that comes from seeing how pervasively and stubbornly we work to take care of ourselves, how we arrogantly refuse to trust God, who offers himself as our protection. And an inside look opens the door into the dark room of terror, where we try to live as men and women without any guarantee that things will work or that we'll be affirmed as adequate or that we'll enjoy the thrill of acceptance.

An inside look, as I have just defined it, is understandably hard to market. It doesn't sound appealing. Why face what makes us miserable? Why bother with developing a self-awareness that creates nothing but emptiness, guilt, and terror? Why not live more happily on the surface?

These are the questions I address in this closing chapter. I want to suggest that an inside look is unbearably painful *almost* to the end, but that what we finally see brings great joy.

A Painful Cure

I recently completed treatment for skin cancer that required me to spread on my back and shoulders an ointment loaded with a chemotherapeutic agent. My skin specialist told me that the chemical would burn whatever skin was bad while leaving good skin unharmed.

We were both surprised when both shoulders became raw within a week. Had you seen them, you might have thought someone had rested hot irons on my shoulders and left them there till every bit of surface skin was burned away.

One weekend when I was using the prescribed ointment, the burned skin on my shoulders began to scream with extra volume. I made a hurried trip to the emergency room where a physician took one look and said, "You're allergic to the ointment. Stop using it at once. Take these strong steroids to fight your reaction and spread this new lotion on your shoulders to prevent infection and soothe your pain." I did, of course, as I was told.

That was a Saturday. On Monday morning, I returned to the same medical complex for follow-up care from my regular dermatologist. Like the other physician, only a brief look was needed to prompt an opinion. But his diagnosis was different. "This is a normal reaction to the anti-cancer chemical. Severe, but normal. Resume treatment."

Again, I did as I was told. That day I applied the ointment I knew would further burn my already raw skin.

I never before appreciated the agony that burn victims endure. Now we had something in common. The difference, of course, is that burn victims are precisely that: victims of a frightful accident. I, however, freely chose to apply the fiery ointment that caused such pain. Why? Why would I create such suffering for myself?

Two reasons: one, I believed that much of my skin was pre-cancerous and that a short season of severe discomfort now would prevent a lengthy, and perhaps fatal, season of worsening discomfort later; two, when the dermatologist left the room after instructing me to further torch my shoulders, a kindly nurse lingered behind to say, "When all this bad stuff is burned off, you'll be left with new skin as smooth as a baby's cheek."

That helped. *I understood that we were searing away the awful to discover something wonderful beneath.*

The same questions can be asked about taking an inside look. Why would any sane person voluntarily rip off the pleasant veneer of a life that's working relatively well to subject himself to the experience of disappointment, self-criticism, and despair? Even more puzzling, why would someone whose life is *not* working well, someone who is already struggling and unhappy, add to her troubles by facing what will make her feel worse?

➤ ➤ ➤

Sharon is a friend of mine. When I first met her three years ago, she was thirty-four years old. She came to a seminar where I was speaking. During a brief morning break, she pulled me aside and told me she intended to take her life. Something arose within me that I can't explain, something I didn't create or invite. I felt a deep desire that she live. I told her so.

Sharon is a survivor of severe childhood sexual abuse and frequent harassment from family members. She came to Christ at age nineteen through Campus Crusade. When she finished college three years later, she got heavily involved in a well-known church where the singles pastor date-raped her. Within a week, she reported to the senior pastor what happened. She was immediately invited to meet with the elders who, after listening to both her story and the single pastor's version, stated that it was her fault and told her she could no longer serve in the children's nursery. They recommended counseling. The head elder's closing comment was, "Your seductive ways bring shame on the name of Christ." And then he prayed that she would learn to trust Christ's love.

Sharon's father hasn't spoken to her since she was twenty. Her mother sends her a hundred dollar bill about once every two months. From her earliest years, Sharon's pain was so blatant and intense, brought on by such hideous sins committed against her, that had she fully felt her pain it would likely have driven her crazy. It was just too much, like extreme physical pain that only unconsciousness relieves.

And her real sin—a priority commitment to protecting herself from more pain—a commitment that seemed necessary because in her mind, there was certainly no God worthy of trust —felt entirely justified and reasonable. The idea that looking out for her own soul was sinful would have seemed as foolish as making it a crime to dodge a bullet fired by a would-be assassin.

Pain *had* to be denied. Self-protection was a *virtue*, a necessary means of survival. Along with most everybody else, that's how Sharon thought.

> > >

Sharon's story is every person's story: disappointing relationships; unsatisfied longings for what this world cannot provide, desires that can nevertheless not be entirely numbed; self-protective resolve, the determination to never hurt so badly again, to somehow feel at least a little better—a determination that seems necessary, therefore justified and even good, and therefore moral.

Every Sunday morning, churches are filled with aching hearts and resolute wills. Most file out the door with their ache more carefully hidden and their demanding wills better disguised as legitimate. But if Sharon, or any of us, is to experience the healing power of the gospel, we must feel our pain and face our sin. Nothing is more difficult.

But just as smooth skin lies beneath diseased skin, so the basis for real joy is hidden beneath unbearable suffering. First the bad skin must be burned. Labor precedes birth. Life after death. That's always the order since Eden. And pain embraced is proportionate to joy celebrated. People who feel only a little of their disappointment and face only a little of their sin experience only a little of the joy available to them in Christ.

But what is this joy we're after? Where is the smooth skin that is supposed to appear after the bad skin is burned off? Is it nothing more than hope that sustains us through despair? C. S. Lewis spoke of the longing itself as the joy that entices us toward heaven. Certainly there is peace in knowing our worst sins are forgiven and eternal bliss awaits. But is there something more? Is there something more for Sharon?

Something Wonderful

Since the day three years ago when Sharon told me she felt like taking her life, she has been changing from the inside out. The book you're now reading played a significant part in that process, as did a couple of God-sent individuals who incarnated the safe embrace of a gracious God.

Soon after being condemned by the leadership of the church she'd been attending, Sharon relocated several states away to accept a new job and, with some real hesitation, began attending another well-known church, this one somewhat smaller and more charismatic in its theology. After sitting in the back row for several months, each time passing the visitor's registry unsigned to the person sitting next to her, she decided on impulse to sign up for a "healing prayer retreat." The brochure on the welcome center table caught her eye: "Let the love of Christ reach into the depths of your woundedness."

That's exactly what happened. At one point during the weekend retreat, she told the pastor in a private meeting how confused and bitter and lost she felt. She surprised herself when she told him how badly she wanted to have sex with her boyfriend, a single professional man who taught the young-adult Sunday school class at another church in the area.

The pastor, a gentle, balding man in his early sixties, listened quietly to her story. When she confessed her desire to yield to her boyfriend's advances, he placed his hands on her shoulders. She later told me she felt nothing but kindly strength. His eyes never dropped, his hands never roamed. Years later, she could quote the pastor's words verbatim: "I hope you don't sleep with your boyfriend. But whether you do or not, there is always a way back to God. I want to help you find it." It was her first taste of grace.

Sharon says she no longer wants to die, though an indescribable ache is still very real. She says she wants to live, to enjoy sunsets and people and more growth. She says she doesn't love her father, though now she wants to. She has a hard time trusting her heavenly Father after all her terrible experiences with her biological dad and a variety of father figures who badly used her, but she is aware of a longing to rest in truly loving arms. And she's pretty sure the arms she wants to hold her belong to God. The longing, she says, feels *strangely like joy*.

She says she feels the natural determination to protect herself from further pain and is sometimes obsessed with relieving the pain she carries with her. When that pain threatens to tear her apart, she finds herself wanting to stand up in church and scream, "Why are you all pretending your life is so together? You hurt, too!" She says she doesn't fit in very well with packaged Christians whose lives are wrapped so nicely.

Yet she finds herself wanting to do nice things for people, even well-wrapped Christians. "Sometimes Jesus' love is just so real, so absolutely overwhelming that I just want to love everybody. I can even pray for my father when that happens; I mean really pray. I *make* myself pray for him a lot but sometimes a genuinely loving prayer just comes out of me. Do you honestly believe heaven is real and that I'm going to get a hug that will last forever? 'Cause if that isn't true, I'm out of here. But if it is, I think I can actually hang on—and even enjoy whatever is enjoyable while giving something to others. I'm actually starting to think I have something to give that's good! After all these years of hating myself, you can't imagine how good that feels."

Sharon is changing from the inside out. She is discovering that beneath the disappointment and sin and terror and agony there is something wonderful.

I do not want you to finish reading this book thinking you are nothing more than a malignant mass of insecurity who must every day beg God not to throw you away in disgust. I do intend that an inside look will expose the arrogance in all of us that insists on handling the difficulties of life in our own strength with neither humility nor trust. But I do not intend that an inside look will leave us thinking we are *no more than aching, demanding people,* or that pain and sin define us.

Before you close this book, I yearn for you to know that the Spirit of God has placed something alive and clean and good and whole in the heart of every Christian. We are now wonderful, unique, terrific people. The actual life of Christ is now in us, infused into the center of who we are, waiting to be poured out toward God in profound worship and toward others in healing grace. That's what God has done for us under the terms of the new covenant.

Yes, we are impossibly foolish, obsessively self-preoccupied, arrogantly self-sufficient, and badly hurting. To deny it ruins the wonder of what Christ did for us when He died. But we are more. By the grace of God, *we are more.* There is good stuff beneath the bad. And yet we often fail to find it because we lack the courage to face the bad stuff that hides it from view.

Releasing the New Life Within

Many of us live our entire lives without ever tapping into the "good stuff," without ever seeing our weathered, cancerous skin become smooth as a baby's cheek. Because we refuse to apply the ointment that burns off the diseased crust, we settle for natural goodness, for the nice things we do that Christians and nonChristians alike are capable of choosing. We seldom experience supernatural goodness, the release of the energy of Christ that is deposited deeply within us through salvation. Just as gold lies beneath rock, the holy desires of our new hearts lie beneath the self-protective demands of the flesh. That gold must be mined if we are to experience joy.

If you long to discover the energy of Christ within you, to change from the inside out by releasing the new life in your soul, then you must do three things: (1) *surrender* to God, (2) take an inside look in the *safety* of loving community, and (3) develop the spiritual *sensitivity* necessary to recognize the promptings of God's Spirit as He stimulates the godly desires of your new heart.

Surrender

By an act of your will, surrender yourself fully to Christ. Determine that you will follow Him no matter what the cost.

Safety

Find a few relationships in which you are willing to risk believing that you are safe from rejection, brutal exposure, or abandonment. Look for a small group where you feel safe enough to receive feedback about how you come across. Let a few grace-filled people help you take an inside look.

Sensitivity

Through the regular spiritual disciplines of solitude and silence, of prayer, meditation, journaling, and fasting, ask God to develop within you a sensitivity to the deepest realities in your Christ-inhabited heart. As you dig through the rocks of pain and sin, as you see how you affect people badly and how unwilling you are to feel difficult emotions, expect to find hidden gold. It's there; the new covenant guarantees it. When you find it, rejoice; nourish those holy desires, risk yielding to them, give what is good within you to others, even when they respond poorly. Believe that the good within you is powerful, that it can advance God's work in someone else's life, and that pouring what is most alive within you into others brings healing to the receiver and joy to the giver.

Three things keep me from cynically giving up on the hope of finding life-changing reality in Christ: Scripture, the Holy Spirit, and a few people. The Scriptures report that Moses related to God face to face; Paul pressed on with the consuming goal of knowing Him; and Peter knew an inexpressible joy. These men (and others) walked a path that changed them into solid people who banked everything on God. The Bible points consistently to the possibility of knowing a God who delights in our fellowship and touches us with transforming power. That possibility gives me endurance. To give up the hope of meeting God would require me to deny the Scriptures, the Scriptures that teach I now have a disposition at the core of my being to love God.

The Holy Spirit has demonstrated His ability to penetrate my soul with ruthless exposure of all that I am and then to comfort or encourage, convict or prod. I know what it is to catch a glimpse of the reality of God that overwhelms me with His majesty, His holiness, and His love. In the middle of the toughest times, I have tasted the goodness of God. That goodness is now inside me, more defining of who I really am than all the badness and hurt that remains.

Several friends have deeply encouraged me with their integrity. I sense the reality of God when I'm with them. When they speak, the words come from deep parts of their souls. Their love is unfeigned—not perfect, but sincere.

The witness of the Scripture, the Spirit, and a few Christians persuades me that there really is a path to knowing God in the midst of any circumstance. If you're a Christian eager to walk that path, then recognize you must make a choice to live life honestly. And know that an honest look at life will produce confusion about what you see in your world and in yourself. It will cause disappointment in others, often at critical moments when a sensitive response would mean so much. And it will provoke conviction over the inevitable ways you violate the command to love.

Confusion, disappointment, and conviction: Is that the path to joy? Or is it a detour into self-preoccupying gloom that encourages an arrogant disdain for all those "shallow" people who lack the courage to be honest about life—and thereby manage to remain happy?

If something is from God, it will inevitably promote the character of Christ in those who embrace it. Confusion should lead not to bitterness and discouragement, but to faith. God is still at work, requiring nothing of us we cannot do, moving through the wreckage of our lives to achieve His good purposes. Our faith is often weak, but the kind of faith that develops to support us through times of overwhelming confusion is strong and resilient.

Disappointment can paralyze us so thoroughly that we won't move toward people for fear of getting hurt again. When we're a victim of shabby treatment by Christians, when our kids live on the edge of disastrous mistakes, when churches and Christian organizations are too busy with "God's work" to care about people's lives, the temptation is strong to give up on relationships. The problems in developing rich intimacy sometimes seem so great that we find a comfortable distance from others and refuse to budge.

But disappointment can drive us to hope. If we remain aware of all our hearts long for, even when we're badly hurt, then the prospect of one day being with Christ can become an alluring passion, a solid anchor that keeps us steady in the worst storms of rejection. A hope that keeps us going when we feel most alone will take over the central place in our affections.

Conviction over lack of love can run deep. If we limit our awareness of sin to such things as obvious moral failure and undisciplined living, we will tend to become rigidly good people whose best relationships remain stiff. We will not learn to love. But when we become sensitive to the subtle violations of love involved in our self-protective style of relating, we'll feel overwhelmed with personal sinfulness.

The realization that every moment consists of a moral choice to look after self or to put others first is staggering. Many of us never wrestle with morality at that level. We prefer to talk warmly of esteeming others above ourselves while carefully avoiding the self-awareness that would convict us about our failure to do it. But when we face our sinfulness, its sheer ugliness can drive us to profound repentance that opens up a new dimension of love. The love that grows out of deep repentance over self-protective sin is penetrating and rich. And it's already in us as Christians, waiting to be released. That's a guarantee of the New Covenant.

Confusion breeds faith; disappointment drives us to hope; conviction leads to love. The path to maturity requires a commitment to replace false certainty, pretended satisfaction, and smug spirituality with disturbing levels of confusion, disappointment, and conviction, which in turn create the opportunity to develop faith, hope, and love. *And joy.*

Before conversion, your identity was *Sinner*; now it's *Saint*. You still sin, of course, and you struggle every day with the urge to sin. But now you have a new heart that's inclined *toward* God, not *away* from Him. Your truest self thrives on holiness the way a child thrives on peanut butter. Not only is it your *responsibility* to believe God, to hope in His promises, and to love Him more than anyone or anything else; it is your *disposition* to do so.

No matter what your present circumstances, your painful memories, your emotional hurts, your moral failures, your internal struggles, joy is available. Your new disposition to worship and serve God cannot be destroyed, no matter how severe your background. As the Spirit of God empowers you to yield to your supernaturally implanted appetites, you will know joy. If you surrender yourself to God, if you face yourself in the safety of a small community of friends, if you develop a sensitivity to the work of God's Spirit beneath your pain and sin, and if you commit yourself to resisting what's bad and releasing what's good, you will experience joy.

Real change, a change that brings joy inexpressible in its wake, is possible if you're willing to start from the inside out. Sharon adds her "Amen."

AUTHOR

Dr. Larry Crabb is the founder and director of the Institute of Biblical Community (formerly the Institute of Biblical Counseling), a ministry committed to training Christians to resolve life's problems biblically and to help others in the context of Christian community.

In addition to conducting IBC seminars across the country, Dr. Crabb teaches courses in the graduate counseling program at Colorado Christian University, Denver, Colorado where he serves as Distinguished Scholar in Residence.

Dr. Crabb earned his Ph.D. in clinical psychology from the University of Illinois in 1970.

Inside Out was Dr. Crabb's sixth book. He has published more than a dozen books, including *Connecting, Finding God, The Silence of Adam*, and *The Marriage Builder*.

Dr. Crabb and his wife, Rachael, live in Morrison, Colorado. They have two adult sons, Keplen and Kenton.

ALSO BY LARRY CRABB

Inside Out Discussion Guide

Thinking of using *Inside Out* in your small group
or Sunday school class? Be sure to get copies
of the companion discussion guide!

Inside Out Discussion Guide

Understanding Who You Are

Life is all about relationships—with God, with others,
and with ourselves. Learn what your relationships
say about you and how to make those relationships
stronger and more intimate.

Understanding Who You Are

Get your copies today at your local bookstore, or call
(800) 366-7788 and ask for offer **#2060**.

pg. 36 most of us make it through
life by coping not changing